Cyrus Thomas

Day symbols of the Maya year

Cyrus Thomas

Day symbols of the Maya year

ISBN/EAN: 9783742827128

Manufactured in Europe, USA, Canada, Australia, Japa

Cover: Foto ©ninafisch / pixelio.de

Manufactured and distributed by brebook publishing software
(www.brebook.com)

Cyrus Thomas

Day symbols of the Maya year

DAY SYMBOLS OF THE MAYA YEAR

BY

CYRUS THOMAS

CONTENTS

	Page
Introductory	203
The first day	207
The second day	215
The third day	221
The fourth day	226
The fifth day	229
The sixth day	231
The seventh day	233
The eighth day	235
The ninth day	237
The tenth day	239
The eleventh day	241
The twelfth day	243
The thirteenth day	245
The fourteenth day	248
The fifteenth day	250
The sixteenth day	252
The seventeenth day	254
The eighteenth day	256
The nineteenth day	260
The twentieth day	262
Appendix.—A list of the deities of the days of the month in the Mani calendar.	265

ILLUSTRATIONS

Plate LXIV. Copies of glyphs from the codices 245
LXV. Copies of glyphs from the codices 246
LXVI. Copies of glyphs from the codices 249
LXVII. Copies of glyphs from the codices 252
LXVIII. Copies of glyphs from the codices 259
LXIX. Shell bearing Maya glyphs 263

DAY SYMBOLS OF THE MAYA YEAR

By Cyrus Thomas

INTRODUCTORY

As the origin and signification of the day and month names of the Maya calendar, and of the symbols used to represent these time periods, are now being discussed by students of Mexican and Central American paleography, I deem it advisable to present the result of my investigations in this line. The present paper, however, will be limited to the days only, as I have but little to add in regard to the month names or symbols. As the conclusion reached by Drs Seler and Brinton in regard to the order and sequence of the days of the month in the different calendars appears to be satisfactorily established, it will be accepted.

As frequent allusion is made herein to the phoneticism or phonetic value of the written characters or hieroglyphs, it is proper that the writer's position on this point should be clearly understood. He does not claim that the Maya scribes had reached that advanced stage where they could indicate each letter-sound by a glyph or symbol. On the contrary, he thinks a symbol, probably derived in most cases from an older method of picture writing, was selected because the name or word it represented had as its chief phonetic element a certain consonant sound or syllable. If this consonant element were b, the symbol would be used where b was the prominent consonant element of the word to be indicated, no reference, however, to its original signification being necessarily retained. Thus the symbol for cab, "earth," might be used in writing $Cauac$, a day name, or $cabil$, "honey," because cab is their chief phonetic element.

In a previous work[1] I have expressed the opinion that the characters are to a certain extent phonetic—are not true alphabetic signs, but syllabic. And at the same time I expressed the opinion that even this definition did not hold true of all, as some were apparently ideographic, while others were simple abbreviated pictorial representations. In a subsequent paper[2] I expressed substantially the same opinion, and gave as my belief that one reason why attempts at decipherment have failed of success is a misconception of the peculiar character of the writing, which peculiarity is found in the fact that, as it exists in the codices and inscriptions, it is in a transition stage from the purely ideographic to the phonetic. I stated also my belief that the writing had not reached the stage when each sound was indicated by a glyph or sign.

[1] Study of the Manuscript Troano, pref. p. vili.
[2] American Anthropologist, Washington, July, 1893.

This may further be explained by the following illustration: The conventionalized figure of a turtlehead is the symbol for a "turtle," *ak*, *ac*, or *aac* in Maya; and a conventionalized footprint is the symbol for "step" or "road," *be*, *beil*, in Maya. These may be brought together to form the word *akyab* or *kayab*, which may have no reference to the original signification of the combined symbols. These two glyphs are, in fact, combined to form the symbol for the month *Kayab*.

These statements will perhaps suffice to make clear my views on this question, which do not appear to have been clearly understood, possibly because of my frequent use of the words "phonetic" and "phoneticism," and perhaps rather loose reference to "letter elements."

It is proper, however, to add that I am inclined to the opinion that modification in the form and details of a glyph which belongs to the class which, for want of a better term, we may designate "phonetic," in many cases indicates a modification or change in the signification or word value. I say in "many cases," because these modifications are due often to the greater or lesser accuracy with which the glyph is drawn, the caprice of the scribe, and other causes which have no reference to sound or signification. For example, the change of a rounded or circular symbol to a face figure, as is often done, does not appear, at least in the day signs, to have any significance. On the other hand, a slight variation, if permanent, may be indicative of a difference in signification or phonetic value. This appears to be true, to some extent, whether we consider the characters ideographic or as, in some sense, phonetic.

The lists of the days in the Maya, Tzental, Quiche-Cakchiquel, Zapotec, and Nahuatl, in the order usually given, are as follows:

Names of the days in the different calendars

Maya	Tzental	Quiche-Cakchiquel	Zapotec	Nahuatl
Imix.	Imox.	Imox.	Chilla.	Cipactli.
Ik.	Igh.	Ik'.	Gui, Ni, Laa.	Ehecatl.
Akbal.	Votan.	Akbal.	Guela.	Calli.
Kan.	Ghanan.	K'at.	Guache.	Cuetzpallin.
Chicchan.	Abagh.	Can.	Ci, Xilla.	Cohuatl.
Cimi.	Tox.	Camey.	Lana.	Miquiztli.
Manik.	Moxic.	Queh.	China.	Mazatl.
Lamat.	Lambat.	Canel.	Lapa.	Tochtli.
Muluc.	Molo.	Toh.	Niza.	Atl.
Oc.	Elab.	Tzi.	Tella.	Itzcuintli.
Chuen.	Batz.	Batz.	Goloo.	Ozomatli.
Eb.	Enob.	E, Ee.	Pija.	Mallinalli.
Ben, Been.	Ben.	Ah.	Quii.	Acatl.
Ix, Hix.	Hix.	Balam.	Eche.	Ocelotl.
Men.	Tziquin.	Tziquin.	Naa.	Quauhtli.

Maya	Tzental	Quiche-Cakchiquel	Zapotec	Nahuatl
Cib.	Chabin.	Ahmak.	Loo.	Cozcaquauhtli.
Caban.	Chic.	Noh.	Xoo.	Ollin.
Edznab.	Chinax.	Tihax.	Gopaa.	Tecpatl.
Cauac.	Cahogh.	Caoc.	Appe.	Quiahuitl.
Ahau.	Aghual.	Hunahpu.	Lao.	Xochitl.

THE FIRST DAY

Maya, imix (or ymix); Tzental, imox or mox; Quiche-Cakchiquel, imox or mox; Zapotec, chilla or chiylla; Nahuatl, cipactli.

The symbol of this day, which is quite uniform in the day series of the codices, is shown in plate LXIV, 1.[1] In this the essential features appear to be the black spot at the top, the semicircle of dots around it, and the short perpendicular lines in the lower half. The form on the right side of the "Palenque tablet," and also in the Lorillard City inscription, copied by Charney, is given in plate LXIV, 2. The only particular in which this differs from the other is that the little circle at the top is crosshatched. The form shown in LXIV, 3, is found in the Tikal inscription; it shows also the crosshatching in the little circle at the top. This character, however, when combined with other glyphs, and when used otherwise than as a day symbol, sometimes varies from the types given. For example, in the symbol of the month Mac it is as shown in plate LXIV, 4. In this a minute, divided oblong, takes the place of the dark spot at the top, and a double curved line accompanies the circle of dots. Another form is shown in plate LXIV, 5. The only variation in this from the usual type is the introduction of two or three minute circles in the curved line of dots and the divided oblong. Dr Seler is inclined to believe that these are essential variants from the true imix symbol; nevertheless, as m is the chief consonant element both in imix, or mox and mac, there appears to be a relation between the form of the glyphs and their phonetic value.

Drs Seler and Schellhas believe im to be the radical of imix and imox, which are dialectal variations of the same word. Dr Brinton, however, basing his opinion on the fact that mox and moxk are used sometimes as equivalents, decides that the radical syllable is m-x. In this he is probably correct, and if so, this furnishes additional evidence of the close relation between form and sound, as in one case m-x are the chief phonetic elements and in the other m-c. It is probable that Drs Schellhas and Seler were led to their conclusion by the fact that the symbol bears a close resemblance to the conventional form of the female breast, which in Maya is im. This, which was perhaps the origin of the symbol, was probably selected simply because m is its only prominent ele-

ment. Nevertheless, it is worthy of notice that the symbol for the day
Ix is frequently represented as shown in plate LXVI, 36, from Tro. 5*c.
This is similar in some respects to the Imix symbol, and the name contains the i and x of the latter. If the writing is phonetic, the points of
resemblance may have some significance, otherwise they do not.

In a previous paper[1] I suggested that the probable signification of the
character LXIV, 7, from Dres. 14c and 40b, is maax, "monkey, ape, imi-
tator." Below the text in each case is seen a dark male figure (or deity),
to which it undoubtedly refers, as is conceded by Drs Schellhas and
Seler. The face character, which forms part of the glyph, may be only
a determinative; at least I am unable to assign it any other value in
this connection, and the necessity for such determinative is apparent.
Brasseur, under ekab-maax, speaks of a phantom or hobgoblin of this
name, which he says signifies "the great monkey of the night." Perez
gives as definitions "duende" (elf or hobgoblin) and "mico nocturno."
Henderson, who writes the name ekabmaax, simply says "sprite, phantom." It would seem, therefore, that among the superstitious beliefs
of the Maya was that of a night phantom or deity, which took the
form of a monkey. But this black figure appears to be different from
those on Tro. 34*–31*, with which Seler connects it and to which he
applies the name Ekchuah.[2]

In the paper above referred to, I have interpreted the symbol shown
in plate LXIV, 8 (from Dres. 35c) taanch, "the crow," assuming the bird-
head to be a determinative. Seler concludes that the bird which this
represents is "a substitute, colleague, or symbol of the Rain god Chac,"
the so-called Maya Tlaloc so frequently represented in the codices.
Although there is in this case no bird figure below to confirm our
interpretation, yet it appears to be justified by the comparisons given
and by its agreement with the phonetic value of the imix symbol. It
is also further confirmed by the two glyphs shown in plate LXVIII,
13, 14, which occur together in Dres. 38b. In this case the two characters, which are combined in plate LXIV, 8, are separated, yet must have
the same signification. Here the bird figure (a man with a bird's head
or bird mask) is seen below. In both instances rain is represented,
showing that the bird is supposed to bear some relation thereto. But
it is more likely that it has direct reference to the wind which accompanies the rain storm rather than to "fruitfulness," as Seler supposes.
Be this, however, as it may, our rendering of the imix symbol in this

[1] American Anthropologist, July, 1895, p. 254.

[2] There appears to be much confusion among writers who have referred to this subject in regard to
the "Black Deities" of the codices. Dr Brinton's remarks on this subject in his late work, "A
Primer of Mayan Hieroglyphics," does not clear up the confusion. Apparently he has not discovered
that quite a number of these are merely black figures of well-recognized deities not thus usually
colored. It appears also, judging by his statements, that Dr. Brinton has failed to identify the characteristics by which the different deities of this class are to be distinguished. Dr Schellhas, in his
excellent paper "Die Gottergestalten der Maya Handschriften," fails also to properly distinguish
between these deities. Dr Seler, whose profound studies have thrown much light on the Maya hieroglyphs, fixes quite satisfactorily the characteristics of some of these deities, yet he confounds others
which should have been separated.

COPIES OF GLYPHS FROM THE CODICES

connection appears to be justified, and indicates that the symbol is used here for its phonetic value rather than with any reference to its primary signification.

Dr Seler also refers in this connection to the lower line of symbols on Dres. 29-30b (three of which are shown in plate LXVIII, 15, 16, 17); to those shown in plate LXVIII, 18, 19, from Tro. 14c; and those shown in plate LXVIII, 20, 21, from Tro. 11a. He remarks that "in a number of hieroglyphs the character *imix* stands as an equivalent of a peculiar animal head which bears as a distinctive mark the element *akbal* over the eye. Thus in the hieroglyphs enumerating those above mentioned which, standing after the hieroglyphs of the cardinal points, seem to express the deities presiding over them, indeed there appears here on the same animal head, on one hand the character *imix*, on the other the element figure 165" (see plate LXIV, 5).

Although I am unable to interpret satisfactorily the *imix* symbols in the places above referred to, I think it can be made apparent that Dr Seler's explanation is without foundation. For instance, by referring to the plates of the Dresden and Troano codices mentioned, it will be seen that there is nothing whatever that refers to an "animal head which bears the element *akbal* over the eye," unless we suppose it to be in plate LXVIII, 16 (from Dres. 29b) and LXVIII, 21 (from Tro. 11a). There is no figure below or connected with either series to justify this conclusion. It is also certain that plate LXVIII, 21 (Tro. 11a) is not an animal head. Possibly plate LXVIII, 16 (Dres. 29b) may be intended for an animal head, but this is not certain and, moreover, it is not repeated in the series.

Referring to Cort. 27a it will be seen that the compound glyph shown in plate LXVIII, 23 (apparently the same as that on Tro. 11a) is repeated four times in one line, each connected with a cardinal point symbol, and each standing immediately over and evidently referring to a large vessel.[1] It is stated that it was a custom among the Maya during certain religious ceremonies to place a vessel in their temples at each of the four cardinal points.[2] As *cum* and *xamal* are Maya words signifying vessel, we still find in these the *u* sound. It is therefore possible that the similar glyphs on Dres. 29b and Tro. 14 and 15 also refer to vessels. The supposition seems to be strengthened by the fact that connected

[1] Dr Brinton (Primer of Mayan Hieroglyphics, p. 44) claims to have discovered that this hitherto supposed "vessel" is, in reality, "a drum." As the four (Cort. 27a) are without any accompaniments to indicate their use as drums, and as each has above it one of the cardinal point signs, there is nothing, aside it to be the form, to lead to the supposition that they are drums. In the same division of the two preceding and three following pages we see vessels of different kinds represented. In the lower divisions pages 21 and 28, are vessels somewhat of the same elongate, cylindrical form, borne on the backs of individuals; and also in the lower division of page 34 are four tall cylindrical vessels, in each of which the arm of a deity figure is thrust. This section is copied in Dr Brinton's work with the subscript "The beneficent gods draw from their stores." Additional proof, if any is needed to show that these are vessels, is found in the Tro. Codex. On plates 8* and 9* are tall cylindrical vessels with the same inverted V marks on them; moreover, one of them has the upper portion margined by the same tooth-like projection as those in the Cortesian plate. That these are vessels of some kind is apparent from the use the pictures show is made of them.

[2] See Brasseur's Lexicon under *kaxab*, also the mention below, under the day 11, of four vessels.

with the former are figures of the four classes of food animals—quadrupeds, birds, reptiles (iguana), and fishes. The latter refer to the hunter's occupation, being accompanied by figures of the deer. Landa, in his descriptions of the various festivals, repeatedly alludes to the four Chacs or Bacabs which represent the four cardinal points, and to the different classes of food animals presented where vessels were used. It is therefore more likely that the symbol is used in the places mentioned because of its phonetic value rather than as a substitute for the heads of lightning animals, for which supposed substitution Dr Seler admits he can not account.

Dr Seler refers also to the glyph on which the long-nose deity is seated, Dres. 44a, shown in our plate LXVIII, 23. The prefix he interprets by "man, human being," and supposes the whole glyph refers to the attributes of the Rain god. As the deity holds a fish in his hand, and is seen in the lowest division of the same plate in the act of seizing fish, is it not more likely that this symbol should be rendered by *cayom*, "a fisherman"? This is appropriate and retains the phonetic value of the *Imix* symbol.

In the compound glyph 24, plate LXVIII, from Dres. 67b, to which Seler also refers in the same connection, we see in the figure below the same deity wading in water in which a fish is swimming. The right portion of the symbol is the same as the last (plate LXVIII, 23) and presumably has the same signification—*cayom*, "a fisherman," or *cayomal*, "to fish." I am unable to interpret the first or left-hand character; possibly it may be found in one of the terms *chuay*, or *cauay*, which Henderson gives as equivalents of *cayomal*. The latter—*cauay*—would give to this prefix precisely the phonetic value I have hitherto assigned it.

The next character Dr Seler refers to in this connection is that shown in plate LXVIII, 35, from Dres. 40a, where the long-nose god is seen below rowing a boat on the water. The adjoining symbol in the text is a fish. It is probable therefore that substantially the same interpretation is to be given here.

The group shown in plate LXIV, 9, consisting of an *Imix* and *Kan* symbol, is of frequent occurrence in all the codices. The relation of the characters in this combination varies, the order being frequently the reverse of that given in the figure, and again one being placed on top of the other. They frequently follow deity symbols, especially the symbol of the so-called "Corn god," and in these instances seem to refer to some attribute of the divinity indicated. However, they are by no means confined to these relations, being found quite frequently in other connections. The combination is occasionally borne upon the back of an individual, as Dres. 16n, and on Tro. 21b it is on the back of a dog. Dr Seler concludes "that it denotes the copal or the offering of incense." However, he subsequently[1] expresses the view that it may signify "beans and maize." In a previous work[2] some reasons were presented by me for

[1] Zeitschrift für Ethnologie, p. 115.
[2] A Study of the Manuscript Troano, pp. 49 and 66.

believing this combination was intended to denote bread or maize bread. This belief is based on the statement by Landa in his account of the sacrifices at the beginning of the year *Mulac*, that they made "images of dogs, in baked earth, carrying bread on the back," and the fact that in plate 91 of the Codex Tro., representing the sacrifices of this year, we see the figure of a dog with this *Kan-Imix* group on its back. This figure (plate LXIV, 10) probably represents the images of which Landa speaks, and the symbols on the back, bread or food in the general sense. Further notice of this combination will be given under the fourth day, *Kan*.

The character shown in plate LXVIII, 26, from Tro. 20*d. is erroneously given by Seler as an example of the *kan-imix* symbol. The two glyphs on the mat figure are unquestionably *imix* symbols, though of the two different types shown in plate LXIV, 2 and 3. He suggests that here it replaces the deity symbol, but this is contradicted by the fact that in both groups where it appears the deity symbol is present. The mat-like figure, which is probably a determinative, shows that it refers to the sack, bag, or kind of hamper which the woman figured below bear on the back, filled with corn, honex, etc. As *xexew* signifies "portmanteau, bag, sack, etc," *xexeab* "a bag or sack made of sackcloth," and *xexebench* "to carry anything in a sack or folded in a shawl," it is more than probable we have in these words the signification of the symbol. The duplication of the *imix* symbol may be to denote the plural; or, as the words come from a root signifying "secret, hidden, covered," it may be to intensify. It is noticeable also that the latter or right-hand *Imix* symbol is similar to that used for the month *Mac*.

In the right section of Dres. 41b is the glyph shown in plate LXIV, 11, which, according to the phonetic system that appears to prevail in this writing, may be translated *yalpolic*, from *yalpol*, "to smooth or plane wood," or, as given by Henderson (MS. Lexicon), "to smooth, plane, or square timber, to bevel off the log." This interpretation, which is given here merely because of its relation to the symbol which follows, is based in part on the following evidence: The left character, which has *yax* its chief phonetic element, is the same as the upper character in the symbol for the month *Yax* (plate LXIV, 12), and also the upper character of the symbol for the month *Yaxkin* (plate LXIV, 13). Other evidence of its use with this value will be presented farther on, and also in reference to the right character of the above-mentioned symbol (plate LXIV, 11), which has been given *p* as its chief phonetic element. By reference to the figure below the text the appropriateness of this rendering is at once apparent, as here is represented an individual in the act of chipping off the side of a tree. This he appears to be doing by holding in his left hand an instrument resembling a frow, which he strikes with a hatchet.

The character immediately below the one above mentioned and belonging to the same series is shown in plate LXIV, 14. It may be interpreted *xexxekah*, "to make flat by repeated strokes." The phonetic value of the parts is obtained in this way. The upper character with two wings is Landa's *ma*, except that the circular wings contain the lines or strokes which the bishop has omitted, and which appear to indicate the *m* sound and are observed in the *Imix* symbol). Colonel Mallery, comparing this with the sign of negation made by the Indians and that of the Egyptians given by Champollion (our plate LXIV, 15), concludes that it is derived from the symmetrically extended arms with the hands curved slightly downward. This will furnish an explanation of the strokes in the terminal circles. The left of the two lower characters is almost identical with the symbol for the month *Mac* (plate LXIV, 4), omitting the *ca* glyph. The lower right-hand character is similar to the symbol for the month *Chuen*. We thus obtain legitimately the sounds *ma ma-ch*, whether we consider the parts truly phonetic or only ikonomatic.

For further illustration of the use of this symbol and evidence of phoneticism, the reader is referred to the article in the *American Anthropologist* above mentioned.

The fact that a symbol is used to denote a given Maya day does not prove, supposing it to be in any sense phonetic, that the Maya name gives the original equivalent. It may have been adopted to represent the older name in the Tzental, or borrowed from the Zapotec calendar and retained in the Maya calendar for the new name given in that tongue. However, the symbol for this first day, which has substantially the same name in the Maya and Tzental, appears to represent the name in these languages and to be in some degree phonetic, *m* being the chief phonetic element represented by it. The crosshatching in the little circle at the top, seen in some of the older forms found in the inscriptions, may indicate, as will later be seen, the *x* or *ch* sound, thus giving precisely the radical *m-x*.

It may be said, in reference to the signification of the names of the day in different dialects, that no settled or entirely satisfactory conclusion has been reached in regard to either.

The Cakchiquel word *imox* is translated by the grammarian Ximenes as "swordfish," thus corresponding with the usual interpretation of the Mexican *cipactli*. Dr Seler thinks, however, that the Maya names were derived, as above stated, from *im*. Nevertheless he concludes that the primitive signification of both the Maya and Mexican symbols is the earth, "who brings forth all things from her bosom and takes all living things again into it." If we may judge from its use, there is no doubt that the Mexican *cipactli* figure is a symbol of the earth or underworld. The usual form of the day symbol in the Mexican codices is shown in plate LXIV, 16, and more elaborately in plate LXIV, 17. As proof that it indicates the earth or underworld, there is shown on plate 73 of the Borgian Codex an individual, whose heart has been torn from his breast, plunging downward through the open jaws of the monster into the shades or earth below. On plate 76 of the same codex, the extended jaws open upward, and into them a number of persons are marching in regular order. These apparently represent the thirteen months of the sacred year. One has passed on and disappeared from view, and the other twelve are following with bowed heads. It would seem from these to be not only symbolic of the earth or hades, but also to have some relation to time.

For positive proof that it is sometimes used to denote the earth, or that from which vegetation comes, it is only necessary to refer to the lower right-hand figure of plate 12, Borgian Codex. Here is Tlaloc sending down rain upon the earth, from which the enlivened plants are springing forth and expanding into leaf and blossom. The earth, on which they stand and from which they arise, is represented by the figure of the mythical *Cipactli*.

It is quite probable that the monster on plates 4 and 5 of the Dresden Codex, which appears to be of the same genus, is a time symbol, and also that on plate 74 of the same codex. It is therefore more than likely that the animal indicated by the Mexican name of the day is mythical, represented according to locality by some known animal which seems to indicate best the mythical conception. Some figures evidently refer to the alligator, and others apparently to the iguana; that on plates 4 and 5 of the Dresden Codex is purely mythical, but contains reptilian characteristics.

Dr Brinton, probably influenced to some extent by the apparent signification of the Nahuatl name and symbol, explains the other names as follows:

This leads me to identify it [the Maya name] with the Maya *ace* or *acac*, which is the name of a fish (the "*pez arma*," "un pescado que tiene muchas brazas"), probably so called from another meaning of *ace*, "the beard." . . . This identification brings this day name into direct relation to the Zapotec and Nahuatl names. In the former, *chipile*, sometimes given as *pi-chilla*, is apparently from *N-chilin-tao*, water lizard, and Nahuatl *cipactli* certainly means some fish or fish-like animal—a swordfish, alligator, or the like, though exactly which is not certain, and probably the reference with them was altogether mythical.

Dr Seler, in his subsequent paper, gives the following explanation of the Zapotec name *chilla* or *chijlla*:

For this I find in the lexicon three principal meanings: One is the cubical bean (wurfel bohne). "Pichijlla, frezolillos o haves con que echan las suertes los sortilegos" [beans used by the sorcerers in casting lots or telling fortunes]; another meaning is "the ridge" (pichijlla, lechijlla, chijltatani, lomas o cordillera de sierra); another is "the crocodile" (cocodrilo, lagarto grande de agua); and another "sword fish" (pella-pichijlla tao, espadarte pescado). Finally, we have chilla-tao, "the great Chilla," given again as one of the names of the highest being. Here it seems to me that the signification "crocodile" is the original one, and thus far suitable. For the manner in which the first day character is delineated in Mexican and Zapotec picture writing [our plate LXIV, 16] shows undoubtedly the head of the crocodile with the movable snapping upper jaw, which is so characteristic of the animal.

Attention is called to the apparently closely related word as given by Perez—*aac*, *kaaac*, "lagartija."

It will not be out of place here to refer to a superstition pervading the islands of the Pacific ocean, which seems strangely coincident with the conception of the physical symbol of this day. This is a mythological monster known in some sections by the name *Taniwha*, and in others as *moko* or *mo'o*.

Dr Edward Tregear[1] speaks of it as follows:

Taniwha were watery monsters generally. They mostly inhabited lakes and streams, but sometimes the sea. Sometimes the beast was a land animal, a lizard, etc., but the true taniwha is a water kelpie.

Mr Kerry Nicholls,[2] speaking of these monsters, says:

With the other fabulous creations of Maori mythology were the taniwha or evil demons, mysterious monsters in the form of gigantic lizards, who were said to inhabit subterranean caves, the deep places of lakes and rivers, and to guard tabued districts. They were on the alert to upset canoes and to devour men. Indeed, these fabulous monsters not only entered largely into the religious superstitions, but into the poetry and prose of Maori tradition.

The Hawaiian *Mo'o* or *Moko* appears, from the following statement by Judge Fornander, to have been applied sometimes to this mythological monster:

The Mo'o or Moko mentioned in tradition—reptiles and lizards—were of several kinds—the mo'o with large, sharp, glistening teeth; the talking mo'o, moo-olelo; the creeping mo'o, moo-kolo; the roving, wandering mo'o, moo-pelo; the watchful mo'o, moo-kaalo; the prophesying mo'o, moo-kaula; the deadly mo'o, moo-make-a-kana. The Hawaiian legends frequently speak of mo'o of extraordinary size living in caverns, amphibious in their nature, and being the terror of the inhabitants.[3]

According to the Codex Fuenleal, at the beginning of things the gods made thirteen heavens, and beneath them the primeval water, in which they placed a fish called *cipactli* (quasea como caiman). This marine monster brought the dirt and clay from which they made the earth, which, therefore, is represented in their paintings resting on the back of a fish.

A similar conception is found both in Malay and Hindu mythology, differing somewhat in details, but always relating to some monster reptile. In the Manek Maya, one of the ancient epics of Java, Anto Bogo, the deity presiding over the lowest region of the earth, is a dragon-like monster with ninety nostrils. The same conception is found also among other peoples.

In the Tonga language *moco* is "a species of lizard;" in Hawaiian *mo'o* or *moko* is "the general name for lizards," and the same word signifies "lizard" in Samoan; *moko-moko* is the New Zealand (Maori) name for a small lizard. Taylor[4] says that *moko-titi* was a "lizard god."

It is therefore evident that a superstition regarding some reptilian water monster prevailed throughout the Pacific islands. It is true also that the Nahuatl *cipactli* certainly means some amphibious or

[1] Jour. Anthrop. Inst., G. B. and I., November, 1888, p. 121.
[2] Ibid., 1885, p. 108.
[3] Polynesian Race, vol. i, pp. 75-77.
[4] Rev. Richard Taylor, Te-Ika-a-Maui; London, 1870.

water animal—a swordfish, alligator, or something of the kind, though exactly which is not certain—or, what is more likely, the reference was altogether mythical.

It is possible, and perhaps probable, as stated above, that the Maya symbol of this day was taken originally from the conventional method of representing the female breast. Dr. Seler and Schellhas appear to be of this opinion. But it does not necessarily follow from this that the character used for the name of the day has any reference to the female breast, as it is more likely used in this relation for its phonetic value alone, as being the chief phonetic element indicated thereby.

If the supposition herein advanced that the combination shown in plate LXIV, 9, denotes bread or food be correct, it is possible that the symbol is also sometimes used to indicate "maize," *irin* or *xim*, on account of its phonetic value. As will be shown further on, the *kan* symbol is not only used to denote the grain of maize and maize in the general sense, but it appears to denote in some cases bread or the tortilla.

THE SECOND DAY

Maya, Ik; Tzental, igh; Quiche-Cakchiquel, II'; Zapotec, *gui, xi, laa, laala or liaa;* Nahuatl, *ehecatl.*

The form of the symbol of this day presents a number of minor variations, the more important of which are shown in plate LXIV, 18-26. Symbol 18 is the form given by Landa; 19-24, those found in the codices; 25 is from the left slab of the Palenque tablet or altar plate, and 26 is from the Tikal inscription.

So far as this character can satisfactorily be interpreted, where used otherwise than as a day symbol, the signification appears to be wind, spirit, or life, whether considered phonetic or not. As illustrations of its use, the following examples are presented:

At the right side of Dres. 72c are the three characters shown in plate LXIV, 27, 28, and 29, which follow one another downward, as shown in the figure, the three forming one of the short columns of the series to which they belong. From the lowest, which is the *ik* symbol, waving blue lines, indicating water, extend downward to the bottom of the division. If these glyphs are considered ideographic and not phonetic, it is still possible to give them a reasonable interpretation. The falling water shows that they relate to the rain storm or tempest. The uppermost character, which appears to be falling over on its side, we may assume to be the symbol of a house or building of some kind;[1] the dotted lines extending from its surface may well be supposed to represent rain driven from the roof. There is, however, another possible interpretation of this character which appears to be consistent with Mexican and Central American mythology. It is that it indicates a house, vessel, or region of the heavens which holds the waters of the

[1] American Anthropologist, July, 1905, pp. 265-261.

upper world. The turning on the side would, in this case, denote the act of pouring out the water in the form of rain. This supposition (although I am inclined to adopt the former) appears to be supported by the fact that this character is used in the Dresden Codex as one of the cloud or heaven symbols, as, for example, on plates 66 and 68. According to Ramirez, the Mexican wind and rain gods occupy a large mansion in the heavens, which is divided into four apartments, with a court in the middle. In this court stand four enormous vases of water, and an infinite number of very small slaves (the rain drops) stand ready to dip out the water from one or the other of these vases and pour it on the earth in showers.[1] As the lowest character in the group mentioned is the *ik* symbol, its appropriate rendering here is beyond question "wind;" therefore, as two out of the three characters, and the rain sign below, indicate the rain storm, we may take for granted that the middle character probably refers to lightning or thunder.

Additional reasons for this interpretation are given in a previous paper[2] and need not be repeated here, as the only object now in view in referring to them is to show that the *ik* symbol is there used to denote wind.

In the third and fourth divisions of plate 26* Codex Troano, five persons are represented, each holding in his hand an *ik* symbol from which arises what appear to be the sprouting leaves of a plant, probably maize (plate LXIV, 30, 31). This is interpreted by Dr Seler as the heart just taken from the sacrificed victim, the leaf-shape figures representing the vapor rising from the warm blood and flesh. It is unnecessary to give here his reasons for this belief, as the suggestion presented below, although wholly different, gives to the symbol in this place substantially the same meaning that he assigns to it, to wit, life, vitality. It is probable that the figure is intended to represent the germination of a plant—the springing forth of the blade from the seed—and that the *ik* symbol indicates plant life, or rather the spirit which the natives believe dwells in plants and causes them to grow. Seler's suggestion that in this connection it may be compared to *kan* is appropriate, but this comparison does not tend to the support of his theory. Take, for example, the sprouting *kan* symbols on Tro. 29b, to which he refers. There can be no doubt that the symbol represents the grain of maize from which the sprouting leaves are rising (plate LXIV, 32). In one place a bird is pulling it up; at another place a small quadruped is attacking it; at another the Tlaloc is planting (or perhaps replanting) the seed.

In the lowest division of the same plate (Tro. 29) are four individuals, three of whom, as may be seen by studying the similar figures in the division above, are anthropomorphic symbols of corn; the other an earth or underworld deity. One of the former holds in his hands a *kan* symbol, which is colored to signify maize; the others hold *ik* symbols. There

[1] Historia de los Mexicanos, as quoted by Brinton.
[2] American Anthropologist, July, 1892.

are two interpretations which may be given this symbolic representation—one, that the *ik* glyphs are intended to denote plant life, that which causes plants to spring up and grow; the other, that they denote wind, which in that country was often destructive to growing corn.

Very distinct reference is made in the "Relacion de la Villa Valladolid"[2] to the injurious effects of winds on the maize crop. It is related in this report, which appears to have been of an official character, made in 1579, that—

From June till the middle of August it rains very hard and there are strong winds; from the latter date the rains are not copious and the wind blows strongly from the north, which causes much mortality among the natives, and Spaniards as well, for they contract catarrh and *barriga* (dropsy?). This north wind destroys the maize crops, which form the main sustenance of both natives and Spaniards, for they use no other bread.

There can be no doubt that most, if not all, of the figures on this plate (Tro. 29) are intended to represent the injurious and destructive agencies to which maize and other cultivated plants were subject. Birds and quadrupeds pull up the sprouting seed and pull down and devour the ripening grain; worms gnaw the roots and winds break down the stalks, one out of four escaping injury and giving full return to the planter. The latter is therefore probably the correct interpretation, the only difficult feature being the presence of the Earth god, which agrees better with the first suggestion.

It is to be observed that the series on Tro. 29c really commences with the right-hand group on 30c. The figure here holds in his hand an *ik* symbol. Following this, the left group on 29c shows a bird pecking the corn; the next, a small quadruped tearing it down; the next, a worm gnawing at the root of a plant; and the fourth, or right-hand group, a corn figure holding a *kan* symbol, indicating the mature grain, the uninjured portion of the crop. It would therefore appear that the *ik* symbol in this series denotes wind.

As additional proof that the symbol is used to indicate "wind," reference is made to Tro. 24a. Here the long-nose Rain god, or Maya Tlaloc, is seen amidst the storm, clothed in black and bearing on his arm a shield on which are two *ik* symbols (plate LXIV, 33), doubtless indicative of the fierceness of the tempest. In front of him is the Corn god, bending beneath the pouring rain. On plate 25, same codex, lower division, the storm is again symbolized, and the *ik* symbol is present here also.

It seems from these facts to be quite certain that the value of the symbol in the codices, so far as it can be satisfactorily determined, corresponds in signification with the Maya name.

Referring again to Dr Soler's theory that the plant-like figures on Tro. 15*, 16* indicate the freshly extracted heart and the vapor arising therefrom, the following additional items are noted: He says that in the text the scene below, or at least these sprouting-plant figures,

[2] Cong. Intern. des Americanistes, Actes de la Quatre Session, Madrid, 1881, tom. 2, pp. 174-175.

are expressed by hieroglyphs 27–29, plate LXVIII. His comparison with the so-called heart figures from the Mexican codices can scarcely be regarded as convincing, for there is hardly any resemblance. Moreover, he omits to furnish an explanation, on his theory, of the fact that some of these rising "vapors" are crowned with blossoms or fruit (plate LXIV, 31).

I think it quite probable that Dr Seler, although not accepting the theory of phoneticism, has been influenced to some extent by the form of the right-hand character of the glyph shown in plate LXVIII, 27. This is much like Landa's *u*, and *ol* in Maya denotes "heart, etc."

According to Brasseur, *olok* signifies "a germ" and "to germinate;" *kolol* also has about the same meaning. This furnishes a consistent and appropriate explanation of the figures, and gives at the same time the phonetic value of the glyph. I have not determined the prefix satisfactorily, but presume it is some word having *ch'* or *t'* as its chief phonetic element, which signifies "little," "plant," or something similar.

I have not determined the other symbols to which Seler alludes in this connection, but some of them, as may be seen by comparison with other passages, do not have special reference to the plant-like figures.

Whether the little sharp-corner square seen in the upper right-hand character of the compound symbols shown in plate LXVI, 28 and 53, and others of similar form, are to be taken as *ik* glyphs is yet an unsolved question. Dr Seler appears to have excluded them from this category in his paper, so frequently referred to, though he subsequently brings them into this relation. But in these places he gives the glyph the signification "fire" or "flame." It is possible that in some of the cases to which he refers he is correct, as, for example, in regard to the figure shown in plate LXVIII, 30, from Dres. 25, where it is in the midst of the blaze. If so, the word equivalent must be *kak*, as it is seemingly a variant of *ik*, and hence may be supposed to have the *k* sound. This will agree with his interpretation of plate LXVI, 29, by *kinichkakmo;* but in this case we must give *ich* as the value of the so-called *ben* symbol. This, however, is not so very objectionable, as there are other places where the chief phonetic element of the *ben* glyph appears to be *i*. It is also to be remembered that it is much like Landa's *i*. It is likewise true, as will hereafter be shown, that the value *ben* does not appear to hold good where it occurs in combination with other symbols. However, until a satisfactory rendering of this little four-corner *ik* (?) symbol in some other place than the fire is found, I am hardly prepared to give full acceptance to Dr Seler's supposition.

The Zapotec names are somewhat difficult to bring into harmony with the others. Dr Brinton's solution is as follows:

In that tongue we have *eti*, air, wind; *chiie*, breath; which we may bring into relation with *gui*: and we find *guiloo*, wind-and-water cloud (halo con vient y agua). Dr Seler prefers to derive *gui* from *guii*, fire, flame, the notion of which is often associated with wind.

It was probably this notion and the fact that the little four-corner ik (?) symbol is sometimes seen in the flame, which caused this authority to believe the symbol denotes "fire," "flame." In the manuscript Zapotec vocabulary by E. A. Fuller, "wind" is *bii*.

Dr Brinton thinks that *ni* is the radical of *nisi*, to grow, increase, gain life. He says:

Lao, or *laolo*, is a word of many meanings, as warmth, heat, reason, or intelligence. The sense common to all these expressions seems to be that of life, vitality.

The form of the Mexican symbol for the day *Ehecatl* (wind), shown in plate LXIV. 34, and also of the mouths of the female figures on plates 26 and 28, Troano Codex, which are emblematic of the storm, appear to be taken from the bird bill. The bird, as is well known, is a wind symbol with many peoples. It has been so esteemed among several tribes of American Indians, and also by peoples of the Old World. As *nii* or *ni* signifies "nose, beak, point" in Maya and several cognate dialects, is it not possible that in this is to be found an explanation of the second Zapotec name? In this case, however, we must assume that the term is borrowed, as in this language *si* or *sia* is the term for "nose." I notice, however, that the name for bird is given as *piguini* and *pigniini*. If *pi* (*bi*) is a prefix, as seems probable from the word for "hen," *gnitii*, then we have some ground for believing that the first Zapotec name has the same fundamental idea as the Mexican symbol.

It therefore would seem that it is not difficult to understand the origin of the Mexican symbol. Examining plate 10, Borgian Codex, which appears to represent the home of the winds, we see that, though mostly furnished with human bodies, they have bird claws as well as bills. But the origin of the Maya symbol is more difficult to account for. Dr Seler remarks:

It is difficult to determine the original idea of this character. Figure 210 [our plate LXIV, 31] and the forms on the reliefs—if we have correctly interpreted these—lead us to think that the wind cross, or the figure of the Tao resulting from it, was the origin of the character. However, the forms of the God, Tro. are not easily reconciled with this.

Dr Brinton[1] asserts, without heeding Dr Seler's caution, that it is the sign of the four directions or four winds—the wind cross—evidently alluding to the sharp-corner square seen in our plate LXVI, 28. But he seems to have overlooked the fact that it is never thus represented in the day symbol. Moreover, no satisfactory proof has been presented showing that this form has this signification. Seler gives it in some places, as above stated, the signification "fire," "flame;" and if his interpretation of plate LXVI, 29 by *Kinich-kakmo* be correct, as Brinton seems to think it is, his interpretations are consistent. However, Seler's assertion that "the forms of the God, Tro. are not easily reconciled with this" must be admitted. In the codices this glyph, as this author

remarks, "rather brings to mind the idea of bangiug," often resembling
a bunch of grapes.

I take for granted the symbol, when standing for the day, is not
pictorial or ideographic, but is adopted for its sound value. If this
supposition be correct, then it must be a conventional representation
of something the Maya name of which is *Ik* or that has substantially
this phonetic value. The form of the Mexican symbol, as above indicated, shows that in selecting it reference was had to the bird bill, to
which possibly may have been added the idea of blowing forcibly from
the mouth, a common method of indicating wind. (See for example the
bird-mouth female, Tro. 25b, where the *Ik* symbol is present.) But
it seems impossible to find in the symbol any reference to the bird,
bird bill, or the act of blowing, or in fact anything indicating, even by
a conventionalized figure, wind, air, spirit, or breath. Hence it is
reasonable to conclude that it has been selected only because of the
resemblance in sound of the thing it represents to the name *Ik*. I
would be inclined to believe that the most usual form is the representation of a tooth or two teeth, the name being used for its phonetic
value only, but for the very troublesome fact that I can find no name
for tooth in Maya to sustain this view. If we could suppose it to be a
conventionalized ideogram of an insect, we would obtain the desired
sound, as Perez explains *Ikel* by "bicho, insecto, polilla, gorgojo."
It must, however, be confessed that none of these suggestions are
satisfactory.

The following additional references to the bird as a symbol of the
wind are appropriate at this point.

Not only is the day *Ehecatl* represented in the Mexican codices by a
bird's head, but we see a bird perched upon a tree at each of the cardinal
points on plate 44 of the Fejervary Codex. Birds are also perched on
three of the four trees representing the cardinal points on plate 65 of
the Vatican Codex.

In speaking of the myths of the Muyscas, Dr Brinton [1] says:

> In the cosmogonical myths of the Muyscas, this (alluding to a certain name) was
> the home or source of light, and was a name applied to the demiurgic force. In
> that mysterious dwelling, so their account ran, light was shut up and the world lay
> in primeval gloom. At a certain time the light manifested itself, and the dawn of
> the first morning appeared, the light being carried to the four quarters of the earth
> by great black birds, who blew the air and winds from their beaks.

The Javanese also assigned a bird to each of the cardinal points,
doubtless with substantially the same mythological concept.

Commenting on a passage of the Popol Vuh, in which the name *Voc*
is mentioned, the same author [2] says:

> The name *Voc* is that of a species of bird (Cakchiquel *Vnk*). Coto describes it as
> having green plumage, and a very large and curved bill, apparently a kind of parrot.
> Elsewhere in the myth (page 70) it is said to be the messenger of Hurakan, resting
> neither in the heaven nor in the underworld, but in a moment flying to the sky, to
> Hurakan, who dwells there.

[1] American Hero Myths, p. 222.
[2] Names of the Gods in Kiche Myths, p. 21.

This is unquestionably the wind symbolized as a bird. The name for wind in Maya is *ikay*, and *Vayu* is a Wind god in Hindu mythology. Garud, the Bird deity of the Hindu Pantheon, who plays such an important rôle in the Mahabharata, and is so frequently termed therein "the foremost ranger of the skies," is apparently the Storm god, the equivalent of the Maya *Hurakan*.

We may remark incidentally that a curious coincidence is found in the fact that there appears to be a relation between the wind and monkeys in the mythology both of the Hindu and of the natives of Central America, or at least of Mexico. Hanuman, the Monkey god, who plays such an important part in the Ramayana, was the son of Pavana, the chief Wind deity. According to Brasseur, in his introductory essay to the *Popol Vuh*, it is stated in the Codex Chimalpopoca that the men were, on a day *Ehecatl*, changed by the wind into monkeys. On what peculiar mythological conception this idea is based I am unable to state.

THE THIRD DAY

Maya, *akbal*; Tzental, *votan*; Quiche-Cakchiquel, *akbal*; Zapotec, *guela*; Nahuatl, *calli*.

The form of the Maya character as given by Landa is shown in plate LXIV, 35; those usually found in the codices are presented in figures 36 and 37 of the same plate. A slight variation which sometimes occurs in the Dresden Codex is given in plate LXIV, 38. In figure 39 of this plate circular dots take the place of the teeth. In another variant, shown in figure 40, there is a row of dots immediately below the broken cross line. The forms shown in figures 41 and 42 are from the inscriptions. As will be seen by comparing figures 36 and 38 with plate LXV, 64, this glyph, in some of its forms, resembles somewhat closely the *ahau* symbol, but is generally readily distinguished from it by the wavy line across the face and the absence of the little divided oblong at the top, which is mostly present in the *ahau* symbol. The lower triangle is usually sharp and extends to the top in the *akbal* symbol, while that in the *ahau* glyph is broad or rounded and does not extend to the top.

The signification of the Maya and Cakchiquel names, and also of the Zapotec, is "night" or "darkness." The Tzental name is that of a celebrated hero, which, according to Dr Brinton, is derived from the Tzental word *votan*, "heart" or "breast." This explanation is accepted by Seler, as Bishop Nuñez de la Vega, the principal authority regarding this mythological personage, says that "in every province he was held to be the heart of the village." Dr Seler also adds that "'heart of the village' is in Mexican called *tepeyollotl*, and that is the name of the deity of the third day character, *calli*" (plate LXIV, 40).

The Mexican name *calli* signifies house. The method by which Dr Brinton brings this and the Tzental names into harmony with the idea of darkness or night is as follows:

The house is that which is within, is dark, shuts out the light, etc. Possibly the derivation was symbolic. *Votan* was called "the heart of the nation," and at

Tzoaloyan, in consequence, he constructed, by breathing or blowing, a "dark house," in which he concealed the sacred objects of his cult. In this myth we find an unequivocal connection of the idea of "darkness" and "house."

Dr Seler's explanation is substantially the same; he differs somewhat, however, from Dr Brinton in regard to the derivation of the word *cotux* (or *totun*), as he obtains it from the Maya *ol, uol,* "heart, soul, will, etc," and *tun,* "in the midst," also "surface, level, extent, front." He concludes, therefore, if *votux* signifies heart, that *votux* denotes "the inmost heart" or "heart of the expanse." It is proper, however, to call attention to the fact that Dr Brinton's derivation of the name in his "American Hero Myths" is slightly different from that given in his "Native Calendar," above mentioned. In the former he says *votun* "is from the pure Maya root word *tan,* which means primarily 'the breast,' or that which is in the front or in the middle of the body; with the possessive prefix it becomes *utan.* In Tzental this word means both 'breast' and 'heart.'" It must be admitted that these explanations are apparently somewhat strained, yet it is possible they are substantially correct, as they appear to receive some support from the figures in the Mexican codices.

Plate 75 of the Borgian Codex, which is in fact the lower part of the figure on plate 76, heretofore alluded to, although having reference to the underworld, appears to be in part a delineation of night. The large black figure probably represents night, the smaller star-like figures denoting stars, and the large one the night sun, or moon. The house in the lower right-hand corner, with the black lining, is the house of darkness. The wind symbol above the roof indicates relationship with the winds. Dr Seler interprets these star-like figures as sun symbols, but the number found together on this plate forbids the supposition that they represent suns. Moreover, the association with the dark figure renders it probable that they are here used to denote stars.

There is, however, a lack in these explanations of a connecting link, which seems necessary to render them entirely satisfactory. The name appears to be intimately associated with that for serpent; or perhaps it would be more correct to say that this mythological personage appears to be intimately connected in some way with the serpent. The title of the Tzental manuscript containing the myth was, according to Cabrera, "Proof that I am a Chan," which signifies "serpent." His chief city was *Nachan,* "the house of the serpent;" his treasure house was a cavern. Simply designating him by "the heart of the nation," "heart of the village," does not appear to furnish a full explanation of his attributes or characteristics.

As the symbol of this day is frequently connected with cloud and rain-storm series, as in Tro. 25a, where it appears to be that from which rain is falling, its signification in these places would appear to be "cloud," which carries with it the idea of smoke, shadow, and darkness. This being true, the most likely supposition in regard to the origin of the symbol is, that it was designed to represent the cloud breaking into drops and falling as rain—in other words, the weeping cloud. Such appears beyond question to be its signification in Tro. 23c and in other places in the same and other codices. This supposition is also consistent with the fact that some of the symbols, especially those of the inscriptions (plate LXIV, 42), have dots along the broken line, which may indicate the raindrops into which the cloud is breaking. I am therefore not inclined to accept Dr Seler's supposition that it is intended to represent the opening to a cavern, after the conventional method adopted by the Mexican artists. It is improbable, though not impossible, that the older system may have adopted some features from the younger. Moreover, this supposition on the part of Dr Seler is in direct conflict with his statement in the immediately preceding paragraph. He says:

It is to be observed as applying chiefly to the manuscripts and the reliefs, that the two side points which project like teeth from the inner circle of the character could in nowise have signified teeth. Such an interpretation is contradicted by the occasional change of their position [plate LXIV, 47] and the fact that they also appear now and then exactly like eyes [plate LXIV, 29].

Now the Mexican cavern symbol, as shown in his figures and as given in Peñafiel's "Nombres Geográficos," appears to be the open serpent mouth with teeth and fangs. It is therefore more probable that the symbol was derived as above indicated. Among the Indian pictographs given by Colonel Mallery [1] as representing clouds are those shown in plate LXIV, 43 and 44. An Ojibwa cloud symbol [2] is shown in plate LXIV, 45, in which the circular outline denotes the sky. It seems quite likely that the Maya symbol is intended to convey precisely the same idea. On the left (bottom) of plate 70, Borgian Codex, is a curved or arch-like figure somewhat on the same order as those given. It appears to represent the sky—but darkened sky, indicating night or obscurity. On its upper surface are nine beads, which probably signify the "Nine Lords of the Night." Below it is a black figure. On each side are two figures, the color of the four differing—one blue, another yellow, another black, and the other red. These are probably the regents of the cardinal points.

If this supposition be correct, the symbol is purely ideographic and not phonetic or ikonomatic; but this does not forbid the idea that when used in other combinations it is used phonetically to give the chief sound element of the word indicated by the ideograph. Dr Seler claims, as corroborative of his supposition, that "all symbols which are combined with the name of the third character are to be fully explained through the word 'cavern.'" But it is far more likely that this (so far as it holds good) is due to the fact that the symbol is used because of its phonetic value or its chief phonetic element, ak, which is the same as the chief element of the Maya name for cavern—actun, actan, aktun (Henderson, MS. Lexicon).

If this supposition be correct, it may furnish a clue to the name of the deity whose symbol is shown in plate LXIV, 46. Here the left-hand

[1] Fourth Ann. Rept. Bur. Eth. (1882-83), p. 756.
[2] Schoolcraft, "Indian Tribes," etc., vol. I, pl. 51, No. 18, p. 406.

character is the *akbal* symbol (though not complete) surrounded by a circle of dots. This circle, Dr Seler contends, often indicates flames which consume the object it surrounds, or light which emanates from that object. If the whole is but a simple ideogram, it must be taken, as a whole, as indicating a particular mythological personage; otherwise it is in part phonetic, or given after the Mexican rebus method of denoting names. If not a simple ideogram, this prefix is most probably used in some sense phonetically with reference chiefly to the *k* sound. The circle of dots is used here probably to indicate the vowel sound *u* or *o*. But in making this suggestion I do not by any means intend to suggest that the Maya scribes had reached that stage of advancement where they could indicate each sound by a character. All I wish to assert is that I find in numerous cases characters accompanied by this circle of dots where the proper interpretation appears to be a word having as its prominent vowel element *u* or *o*. Hence the inference that there is some relation between this circle and these vowel sounds—this and nothing more.

In Dres. 16c is the symbol shown in plate LXIV, 49. This, as I have shown elsewhere,[1] represents the *kukulk* or Quetzal figured below the text. Here are encircling lines of dots, and in the Maya name the *k* sound repeated; and here also is Landa's *ku*. In Dres. 47c the symbol for the month *Mol* is given as shown in plate LXIV, 50. Here again is seen the circle of dots, and the vowel appears to hold good in other places. We see it in Landa's first *o*. It will also assist us in giving at least a consistent interpretation to the strange character shown in plate LXIV, 51, which occurs repeatedly on plate 19 of the Tro. Codex. In the pictures below are individuals apparently, and as interpreted by most authorities, engaged in grinding paint or other substance or in making fire. The right half of the glyph, including the circle of dots and cross-hatching might, according to the value heretofore given those elements, be rendered by *hach*, "to rub, grind, pound, pulverize;" which certainly agrees with the interpretation usually given the pictures below. Possibly the whole glyph may be interpreted by *cocolkachak*, "to triturate." While this, so far as it relates to the left portion of the glyph, is a mere suggestion, it agrees with the fact that the ornamented or cross-barred border is found in the symbol for *Cib*, and the three dots with Landa's *c*.[2]

---

[1] American Anthropologist, July, 1895, pp. 241-245.

[2] Dr Brinton (Primer, etc, p. 93) explains it as the symbol of a drum. He remarks that "in a more highly conventionalized form we find them in the Cod. Troano than [giving plate LXIV, 51], which has been explained by Rosny, Thomas, and others as marking fire or as grinding paint. It is obviously the drawing, what I have called the 'pottery decoration' around the figures, showing that the body of the drum was earthenware." Yet (p. 130 and fig. 59) Dr Brinton explains this identical group or paragraph as a representation of the process of making fire from the friction of two pieces of wood. It seems to me clear that this glyph represents something in the picture, and not the personage, as there is a special glyph for this. A comparison of the groups in the two divisions of this plate (Tro. 19) and plates 5 and 6 of the Dresden Codex shows that the glyph refers to the work or action indicated by the picture. That it refers to something is as indicated by the picture, and that no drum is figured, will, I think, be admitted by most students of these codices.

In Tro. 11*d is the character shown in plate LXIV, 52. As the right portion is the upper part of the symbol for *ckikin*, "west" (see plate LXIV, 53), its phonetic value may be a derivative of *kuch, kuchuuki, kuchuk*, "to spin, to draw out into threads." Henderson gives *chuch* as an equivalent. As the suffix in plate LXIV, 48, is the character I have usually interpreted by *u*, this would give us some of the elements of the name *Kakyhua* and not *Itzamna*, as Seler and Schellhas suppose. Possibly, however, the deity represented may be *Buklum-Chaam*, the god adored at Ti-ho and usually considered, though without apparent justification, as the Maya Priapus.

The somewhat similar character, plate LXIV, 55, from Tro. 18*c, which Dr Seler considers synonymous, is probably essentially distinct, as it bears a somewhat stronger resemblance to the *chuca* than to the *aTbal* symbol. In character 54, plate LXIV, from Dres. 17b, which denotes the vulture or rapacious bird figured below the text, it probably indicates the *c* sound, as the most reasonable interpretation of the symbol is *hchom*, "the *sopilote*" (Perez), or *hchuy*, "a hawk or eagle." If the character shown in plate LXIV, 54, is intended to indicate the bird figured below, and is neither of those mentioned, it is probably one the name of which begins with *ch*.

The symbol of the month *Zes* (*Tzoz* or *Zots*) also contains this supposed *akbal* glyph, but in the varied form last above mentioned, which, as we have said, bears a strong resemblance to the *chuca* symbol. This, as will be seen by comparing, bears a very close resemblance to glyph LXIV, 54. If phonetic, we must assume that the *ch* (if the interpretation of the former be correct) has been hardened to *z* or *tz*.[1]

The same character is also found in the symbol for the month *Xul* (see plate LXIV, 56, from Dres. 40c). As Dr Seler refuses to accept the theory that the characters are either phonetic or ikonomatic, he concludes, in the following words, that resemblance in the forms of the symbols indicates relationship in the subject-matter:

Xul signifies the end, the point; *xulel*, to end; *xuleb, xulucah*, to bring to an end; *xulub* (that with which anything ends), horns, or he who has horns, the devil; *xulbil*, jests, tricks, deviltry. We see, therefore, that this word contains doubtless a reference to something unholy, uncanny, demoniac. To the Central Americans the bat was not merely a nocturnal animal. The Popol-Vuh speaks of a Zo'tzi-ha, "bat house," one of the five regions of the underworld. There dwells the *Cama-zo'tz*, "the death-bat," the great beast that brings death to all who approach it, and also bites off the head of Hunapu.

Instead of having to surmise this fancied relation, I think the explanation is to be found in the fact that similarity in the form of the glyph is indicative of a similarity in the sounds of the words represented. Here the *ch* becomes *z* (*zh*).

Dr Seler also calls attention in this connection to the animal figures in Dres. 36a and elsewhere, which are "represented as plunging down

---

[1] Dr Brinton (Primer, p. 121) errs in regarding the *suprefix* to this glyph as the *kin* or *sun* symbol.

from heaven with torches in their paws, and fire also issuing from the tassel-like ends of their tails, which doubtless denote the lightning, the death-dealing servant of the Chac." By the mention of this last word—chac—Dr Seler has shown that correct reasoning by a different line leads to precisely the same result as that which appeals to the phonetic or ikonomatic character of the symbol. Here again the ok sound appears as the chief element of the character. The rain or field deities, the chacs, are usually represented in the codices as dog or panther like animals; and chaac, "the tempest," and, according to Henderson, chac also, signifies lightning. But the relation of figures and phonetic value includes also the animal; chacbolay, "a savage tiger, a young lion" (Perez); chacbcay, "a leopard" (Henderson); chacck, "a leopard;" chaackel, "a tiger, jaguar;" chac-ikal, "the storm, the tempest." The similar figures in Tro. 32c probably symbolize the dry burning season which parches and withers the corn. The word is probably choco, chocou, or some related form.

THE FOURTH DAY

Maya, kan or kanan; Tzental, ghanan; Quiche-Cakchiquel, kat (kate, k'atic, gatic); Zapotec, gueche or gueche; Nahuatl, cuetzpallin.

The Maya symbol of this day is subject to but few and slight variations. The principal forms are shown in plates LXIV, 57, to LXV, 3. That given by Landa is presented in plate LXIV, 57. The forms in the codices are shown in plates LXIV, 58; LXV, 1, 2, 3, that with the eye (LXV, 3) being the usual form given in Peresianus; LXV, 4 represents it as found on the right slab of the Palenque tablet.

The significations of the Maya word kan are various, as "yellow," "rope," "hamac," etc, and, according to Dr Brinton, the Tzental ghanan is the same word under a slightly different form. However, he contends that the original sense is to be found in the Cakchiquel word kan, as given by Guzman (in a manuscript work in his possession), who says it is the name applied to the female iguana, or tree lizard. This, it is true, brings the signification into close correspondence with that of the Nahuatl term, but it is more than probable that the Maya and Tzental terms were in use before the application mentioned by Guzman was made by the Cakchiquel. It is noticeable, however, that in the list from Taylor's "Te-Ika-a-Maui," presented in the appendix, "lizards" are given as symbolic of one of the New Zealand days.

This interpretation, however, savors too much of an effort to bring the signification into harmony with the Mexican name. Moreover, it is difficult to explain the use of the Maya symbol on this theory, as it is undoubtedly frequently employed to denote the grain of maize. For example, it represents the seed from which a corn plant is springing, as on Tro. 20b (see plate LXV, 39); and one figure in the same division represents a bird plucking it up, while another shows some small quadruped seizing it. It is also frequently represented in all the codices

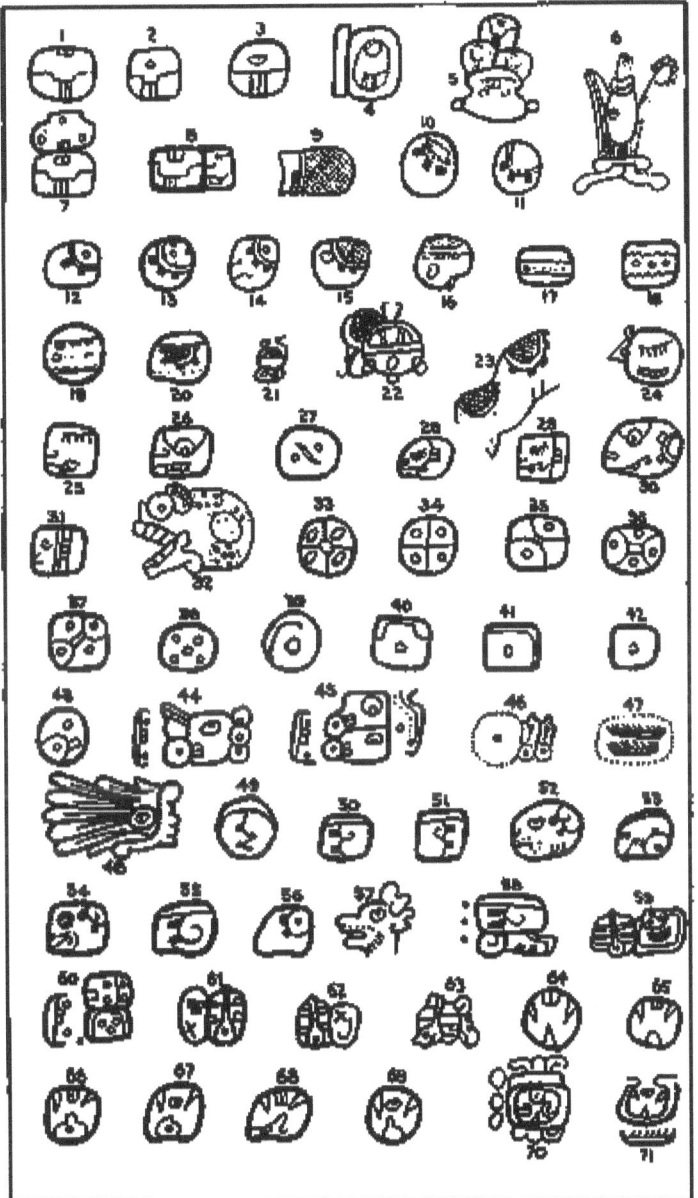

COPIES OF GLYPHS FROM THE CODICES

as on a platter or vessel placed as an offering to some deity, and is often given a yellowish tint in these places. That the plant which arises from the symbol in these instances is the maize stalk is admitted by Drs Schellhas and Seler, although they do not seem to recognize the fact that the symbol represents the grain of maize which gives birth to the stalk. However, Dr Seler, in his subsequent paper above referred to, concludes that it refers to the seed, dropping his former interpretation. Both seem to recognize the whole glyph as a symbol of the stalk. Concerning this, Dr Seler says:

Indeed, we see in Cod. Mexicanus the maize shoot employed to express the word xeuh, "seed." I believe that the character kan repeats the Mexican idea, the maize stalk. This explains for us the reason why the character kan, as above pointed out, always appears among the sacrifices.

I fail to understand why this authority applies the symbol to the "stalk," when it is the fruit, the ear, the grain, which furnishes food, and may therefore be very properly used as the symbol of food.

In plate LXV, 5, is presented a copy of one of these corn offerings as found on Tro. 9*b. As the vessel containing the offering appears to be a vase, pot, or olla, it seems improbable that the offering it contains should consist of maize stalks. It is true, however, that instances occur, as on plates 31–33, Tronno, where the stalk rises from the kan symbols contained in a vessel, but these are evidently given in a figurative sense, as the vessel rests on a serpent. But even here there is evidence that the symbol denotes the grain or ear, and not the stalk, as in the lower right-hand corner of plate 24 a human figure is represented as feeding a bird with the symbol, which can not be construed in this instance as representing the stalk.[1]

Ximenes, who gives the Cakchiquel name as oat, says it refers to a net used for carrying maize, but means "lizard." Dr Seler, referring to this statement, says he strongly suspects that "the Mexican equivalent of this character has furnished him with this interpretation." He adds further that, in his opinion, "it has no connection with the Maya root kax, kaan, 'rope,' 'cord,' 'mat-cord,' and kan—Quiche-Cakchiquel, k'an (gan)—'yellow.'" He believes the Maya term is derived from kaanan, kanan, which signifies "to be superfluous," "overflow," "to abound."

Dr Brinton thinks that the Zapotec gauche, translated by Seler "frog or toad," is more likely a variant of garuche or garuche, "iguana."

It is apparent from these widely different opinions that the signification of none of the names, save that of the Mexican calendar—cuetzpallin, "lizard"—has been satisfactorily determined.

<hr/>

[1] Dr Brinton (Primer, p. 116) says the object represented by this symbol is "a polished stone, shell pendant, or bead." This authority considers the dot or cycle in the upper part as a perforation by which it was strung on a cord. If this be true, it is strange that we see them neither in the endless strung on strings, though necklaces are frequently represented; and that we do see them piled up in vessels, see them putting forth shoots and leaves, and see birds and quadrupeds devouring them. Dr Brinton himself (p. 122, R. No. 20) gives one of these sprouting kan symbols, which he says "is a picture of the maize plant from Cod. Tro., p. 29." That it is not used hieroglyphically here is evident, as kan in Maya is not a name for maize or grain of maize.

In attempting to ascertain the signification of the names of the day, exclusive of the Mexican calendar, it is best to exclude from consideration at first the signification of the latter, and allow it to have no influence in arriving at a conclusion. The attempt by Dr Brinton to force agreement with the latter appears to be unsatisfactory.

I am inclined to agree with Dr Seler that the Maya symbol for the day *kan* and the Mexican symbol for *tecpatl*, "flint," are based on the same fundamental concept, if the flint-like symbols on plate 12 of the Borgian Codex, one of which is shown in plate LXV, 6, are *tecpatl* figures; of this, however, there is considerable doubt. Seler's opinion is based on those of this type. There can be no doubt that here this spindle-shape figure represents the shooting plant, the central stock or stem, or, what is far more likely, the seed which gives birth to the plant. Although they occupy the position of the stock or stem, yet from the form, the fact that some of them have the eye, and that from them the roots stretch downward, I am inclined to believe they are intended to denote the seed. The *kan* symbol, as above stated, is also represented in the codices as that which gives birth to the plant, as that from which the sprouting plant springs. It is probable, therefore, that it was originally taken from the grain of maize, which it fairly represents.

Now it is well known that "yellow" is one of the primary meanings of *kan*, and that the word is closely associated with fruit, the "yellow" referring in a large degree to the ripening fruit, especially of the maize plant. According to Henderson one signification of *kan* is "ripe, as fruit, timber," and, according to Perez, *kankan* is "sazon en [que] las frutas, aunque no estan maduras por estar las que tomando el color amarillo." In Cakchiquel *kan* (*gan*) signifies "yellow, ripe, rich." According to Otto Stoll, *raik* (or *vaack*), which is almost identical with the Zapotec name of the day, is the word for "fruit" in several of the Maya dialects. According to the vocabulary of Cordova, as given by Ternaux-Compans, "yellow" in Zapotec is *nagache*, and in Fuller's MS. Vocabulary it is *na-guichi*, the *na* being a prefix signifying "thing." The anonymous author, however, writes it *bechii*. We also notice that "gold" in this language is *gache*, probably referring to the color. It is likely, therefore, that the Zapotec name of this day signifies "yellow, ripe, mature," referring to fruits, especially maize.

When maize was introduced into New Zealand it was named *kanga*, probably after the Malay *tangkai*, the name for an "ear of corn." The Mextitlan name of the day is *Xilotl*, "an ear of corn," or "a young maize shoot." These facts seem to show that the symbol has some reference to maize, and tend to confirm the view expressed above, that the compound symbol shown in plate LXIV, 9, denotes "maize bread." The presence of the *kan* character in the symbol of the month *Cankin* or *Cankin* or *Humku* (plate LXV, 7) is difficult to explain on the theory that it retains here the signification given it as the symbol of the day *Kan*, whether considered ideographic or phonetic, unless we suppose the name is incomplete and should have *kan* added to it. I am somewhat disposed to believe that it is sometimes used alone to denote bread, and is then to be interpreted by *wah*. Take, for example, the figure in Tro. 30d. Here we see a dog seated on a *kan* symbol, with the same symbol taking the place of the eye. As *yet* is dog in Maya and *yocowh* the tortilla or bread of maize, and the compound glyph in plate LXV, 9, is in the text, this may be an instance of the true rebus method of representing a word. Another instance of a similar character will be given under the day *Oc̆an*. Possibly the *kan* glyph in the month symbol may have there the signification *nak*.

The fact must be borne in mind that this character, as before stated, is often, and perhaps most frequently, used, except where it indicates the day, merely as the symbol of corn or maize. As an example, take the compound character shown in plate LXV, 8, from Tro. 33c. In the picture under the text is the Corn god represented with the dead eye and bound with cords; above his head is a dog-like animal bearing burning torches. This representation, taken in connection with what is seen in the other divisions of the plate, appears, as heretofore stated, to denote the burning drought of summer, which is destroying the maize crop. As the right portion of the compound character is the *cimi* symbol, probably representing death, the whole character very likely indicates the dying corn. I have not found any combination where the rendering of the symbol by *kan* proves satisfactory. In fact, with the exception of the *kan-imix* combination heretofore mentioned, *kan* is very seldom combined with other glyphs, there being only some two or three in the Tro. Cod., and three or four in the Cortesian Codex. It appears, however, a number of times in combination in the Dresden Codex, but as yet I am unable to interpret any of them satisfactorily.

THE FIFTH DAY

Maya, *chicchan*; Tzental, *abagh*; Quiche-Cakchiquel, *can*; Zapotec, *ci*, *ziie* or *guii*; Nahuatl, *cohuatl*.

The forms in which the symbol of this day appears are various and sometimes widely divergent. The principal ones are shown in plates LXV, 9 to 20. The form given by Landa is seen at 9; that most common in the Codex Tro. at 10. Other forms which frequently occur are shown at 11–13; those shown at 14–16 are from the Troano Codex. Some unusual forms which vary widely from the typical glyph are given at 17–20.

The change of a symbol to the face form, as seen in this instance at LXV, 16–19, does not appear to have any significance. The chief element of this character is the circular spot in the right portion, usually bordered by a double line and little square blocks, with the interior generally crosshatched. As the crosshatching is also found in the symbol for the month *Pax* (plate LXV, 22), it is probable, if phonetic, that this characteristic denotes the *x* (sh) or *ch* sound. As a similar marking is frequently present on the serpent figures in the codices (plate LXV, 23), it is possible that its signification is *chan*, "serpent," or it may refer to some real or mythological characteristic.

The signification of the names of this day, except that of the Nahuatl calendar—*coahuatl*, "serpent"—appears to be uncertain. Perez says the word *chicchan* can be explained only by considering it to be incorrectly written for *chichan*, "little." Henderson in his lexicon writes it *chichan*, and gives as the meaning of the word, "new, young, as *chichan* u, the new moon." Dr Seler first suggested that the first part of the name might be derived from the root *chi, chii*, "mouth, to bite," and hence that the signification might be "the biting serpent." However, he subsequently concluded that the proper interpretation is "a sign marked or taken," from *chich*, "a sign or mark," and *ch'aan*, "something taken or carried away." Dr Brinton thinks there is much less difficulty in construing it as *chich*, strong or great, and *chan*, the generic Tzental term for serpent. The generic term for serpent in the Zoztzil is *chan*.

Dr Seler does not attempt an explanation of the Tzental term, but Dr Brinton says that it means in that dialect and in Cakchiquel, "luck, fate, fortune." This, he says, is identical with the Zapotec *oi, zii*, and *guii*, and, as he finds evidence that the serpent is mentioned as an animal whence portents were derived by the Zapotecs, thinks this furnishes the connecting link with the signification in other calendars. This explanation is so circuitous, and in fact strained, as to render it unsatisfactory.

A study of the symbol with reference to its origin may perhaps furnish some aid in arriving at the true signification of the name. As will be seen by reference to the various forms of the symbol, the bordering of the circular inclosed space appears to be more permanent than the inner markings. This is apparent from the fact that the little squares or blocks are retained in all the types except the anomalous forms shown in plate LXV, 16–18, and even in one of these (LXV, 18) they appear. On the other hand, the markings in the inclosed space are varied, and in some instances, as LXV, 11, are omitted altogether. It would seem, therefore, from this that the bordering was considered the essential element of the glyph. From what, then, is the symbol taken? If we turn to Dresden 25c, we see in the priest's robe, in all probability, that from which the symbol was derived. Here we have the inner crosshatching and the little dark blocks or squares around the border. The same pattern is seen also on Tro. 16*b and c, and on the female dresses, some codex, 20*c and d. On the latter, in some cases, is the waved line seen in the unusual forms of the day symbol shown in plate LXV, 17, 18, and 19. Other examples could be referred to, but attention is called only to one more, viz, the curtain-like articles exhibited on Tro. 30*b, where we see not only the inner crosshatching and bordering blocks, but on the side borders the precise marking of the day symbol shown in plate LXV, 17.

As *chi, chii,* signifies not only mouth, but also "limit, border, margin, shore," and especially the "skirt or lower edge of a garment," the relation of the symbol to the name of the day is obvious. It is used here for its phonetic value—*chi.* As *chii* signifies "to bite, prick, to sting as a serpent," and *chan* denotes "serpent," the true explanation of the name of the day would seem to be "the biting or stinging serpent." This will perhaps justify us in supposing that where the symbol is found on a serpent it must have reference to this characteristic.

I had not observed when the above was written that Brasseur had expressed substantially the same view in regard to the origin of this symbol.

THE SIXTH DAY

Maya, *cimi;* Tzental, *tox;* Quiche-Cakchiquel, *camey;* Zapotec, *lana;* Nahuatl, *miquiztli.*

Landa's symbol for this day is shown in plate LXV, 24. The usual form in the Codex Tro. and Cortesian Codex is given in LXV, 25; it is varied frequently by an extension of the line from the mouth, somewhat as in symbol 26 of the same plate, which is the usual form in the Dresden Codex. A variation of this is seen at 29, which seems to have given rise to the unusual form shown in 31. A radical variation is that given at 27. The symbol of the Death god, 26 and 30, is sometimes, though rarely, substituted as the symbol of this day. The closed or dead eye and prominent teeth, as seen in the usual forms, show very clearly that the symbol is simply a conventional representation of the naked skull. The form shown at 27, however, is more difficult to account for; reference to it will be made farther on.

The Maya, Quiche Cakchiquel, and Nahuatl terms signify "death." The Tzental name *tox,* however, presents a difficulty not readily overcome in order to bring its signification into harmony with that of the others. Dr Seler does not attempt an explanation in his paper on the meaning of the day names, and in his subsequent article fails to reach any settled conclusion. Dr Brinton thinks it means something (as a human head) separated, sundered, cut off; "hence *tox-oghbil,* the ax or hatchet; *q-tox,* to split, divide, cut off." In this, he holds, it agrees precisely with the Zapotec *lana,* which, he says, the Zapotec vocabulary renders "a separated thing, like a single syllable, word, or letter." Dr Seler's interpretation of the Zapotec name is wholly different, as he says that the most natural of the various significations given is, in his opinion, "hare;" *pela-pillaana,* "liebre animal;" *too-quixe-pillaana,* or *pella-pillaana,* "red hare liebres." I observe, however, that in Fuller's vocabulary *ga-lana* is "to steal." Other significations are "name," "flesh," "secretly," etc. The proper interpretation of the Zapotec name therefore appears to be very doubtful. In Cordova's vocabulary, as given by Ternaux-Compans, "fleche" is given as the meaning of *quii-taxa*. In Tzotzil *ptox* signifies "to split, break off, break open, to chop." In Maya we have *tok*, which, as a substantive, Perez explains by "pedernal, la sangria;" as a verb it signifies "to bleed, let blood." In this dialect *tox* denotes "to drain, draw off liquor, spill, shed."

The usual form of the Mexican symbol for this day is shown in plate LXV, 32. It is also a naked skull.

Like Dr Seler, I am compelled to admit that I can give no satisfactory suggestion as to the origin of the form shown in plate LXV, 27. According to Colonel Mallery,[1] one sign among the Indians for knife is to "cut past the mouth with the raised right hand," which, if figured, would probably bear some resemblance to the marks on this symbol.[2]

THE SEVENTH DAY

Maya, manik; Tzental, manik; Quiche-Cakchiquel, quei; Zapotec, china; Nahuatl, mazatl.

The symbol for this day, shown in plate LXVIII, 31, is without any change worthy of notice, the only difference observable being a greater or less degree of perfection with which it has been drawn by the aboriginal artist. It is found, however, in various combinations where it is subject to variation in form, if these in truth be intended for this symbol. As Brasseur de Bourbourg has suggested, this appears to have been taken from the partially closed hand, where the points of the fingers are brought round close to the tip of the thumb. Whether intended to show the palm or back outward is uncertain, though apparently the latter. The nearest approach I find among the Indian signs figured by Colonel Mallery is that denoting "little, diminutive, small." But the position of the hand in the symbol appears to indicate the act of grasping; either signification gives *ch* as the chief phonetic element of the Maya word *chaa* and *chichan*, signifying "little," and also, *chuch*, "to grasp, to seize" ("alcanzar, asir, prender," Perez); or *chuuc*, "to take, grasp, catch, seize," Henderson.[3] It would seem from this that if the symbol is phonetic in any sense, the chief element of the word indicated is *ch*. The supposition by Drs Schellhas and Seler that this symbol sometimes contains the elements of the sign of the four winds or wind cross, appears to be without any real foundation. The partial cross-shape figure in it is merely the conventional method of drawing the opening between the fingers, and would be just as correctly given as an oval as an inverted bar.

As this interpretation of the symbol is quite different from that given by other writers, some evidence to justify it is presented here.

[1] First Ann. Rep. Bur. Ethn., p. 396.
[2] The Division (Primer, p. 42) says: "Former students have been unable to explain this design" and suggests that it is a mazgot.
[3] Brasseur follows Brasseur in supposing it represents the "grasping hand," and thinks it is a cohue of mazat, "nely, tomar con los manos."

Attention is called first to the symbol for "west." shown in plate LXIV, 33. The lower portion is the recognized symbol for *kin*, "day" or "sun," and the upper portion is beyond question the *manik* character. As *chikin* is the Maya name for "west," we are justified in assuming that here at least this *manik* symbol is to be interpreted by *chi*, and is in some sense phonetic. As *china* is the Zapotec name of the day, and signifies "deer," and *chigh* is the Zotzil name for "deer," it is probable that the symbol preserves the old name, while in Maya this old name has been supplanted for some reason, or through some linguistic process, by *manik*.

Dr Seler calls attention to the character shown in plate LXVIII, 32, from Dres. 18c, which is repeated in the form LXVIII, 33, on plate 21b. That this refers to the deer figured below must be admitted, as this is clearly shown by the relation of the characters in the adjoining section to the animals figured below the text. Henderson (MS. Lexicon) gives *zolke* as "the mule deer." If this could be considered substantially equivalent to *cholzck* in sound, our *manik* symbol would retain its value. The objection to this supposition is that the figure is probably intended for a doe instead of the male. Brasseur gives *chargue* as the name applied to a small species of deer. It is true these interpretations leave out the numeral prefix; nevertheless they serve to show that it is probable the true name is a word which retains the phonetic value of the *manik* symbol as we have given it. Be the word what it may, two conclusions may be relied on: First, that it alludes to the deer, and, second, that one of its chief phonetic elements is *ch*. The character shown in plate LXVIII, 34, from Tro. 11*b, has probably the same element in its phonetic equivalent, for the Maya verb *hax (haxmaki)*, "to twist or turn by rolling the thing between the palms of the hands; make cord used for muslin or cloth," etc, gives substantially this phonetic equivalent.

The character shown in plate LXVIII, 35, from Dres. 10b, is referred to by Seler as indicating an offering to the gods. In this he is possibly correct. As *tick*, in Maya, signifies an "offering," "a sacrifice," and *tick (tichah)* "to offer, present," etc, it is probable that in this instance also the *manik* symbol retains *ch* as its chief phonetic element. However, I am inclined to believe it refers to the collecting or gathering of the ripened fruit. In this case the prefix must be understood as a determinative indicating piling or heaping up, putting together or in a heap, or storing away. Of the Maya words indicating this operation, we note the following: *Chick (chichah), kich,* and *koch.* each of which has *ch* or *cä* as its chief consonant element. This interpretation agrees very well with the fact that here, as elsewhere, a date is to be taken into consideration. On such a date, at such a time, the cacao is to be gathered, is to be harvested and stored away. Students of these codices, in their attempts at interpretation, appear, as a general thing, to overlook the fact that almost every paragraph or group of glyphs in the script is accompanied by a date which must be taken into consideration in the interpretation. The symbol which follows immediately to the right, shown in plate LXVIII, 36, may be rendered *cacau*, the "caeno," as the duplicated comb-like character is Landa's *ca*.

As the Quiche-Cakchiquel, Zapotec, and Nahuatl names all signify "deer," the difficulty in bringing all into harmony lies in the Maya and Tzental names. Dr Seler's explanation is substantially as follows: That the word *manik* is from the root *man* or *mal*, which signifies "to pass quickly;" *manik* may therefore mean "that which passes by," "that which is fleeting." Dr Brinton gives the same explanation, and concludes that the deer is referred to metaphorically. In regard to the Tzental name *moxic*, Dr Seler suggests that it may be founded on the root *max*, from which is derived *maxax*, "swift." Dr Brinton objects to this derivation, as *maxax* with the signification "swift" is from *ma*, "not," and *xax*, "slow, tardy," and suggests that the name is probably a corruption of the Nahuatl *mazatl*. However, it may be stated in favor of Seler's explanation, that Henderson gives *maxax*, "quickly, shortly, without hindrance," which is apparently another form of *maxax*. Dr Seler, however, concludes, from a study of the relations in which the character is found in the codices, that it is the symbol of offering, of sacrifice, the deer being esteemed the animal most appropriate for this purpose. Henderson says *manik* signifies "calm," evidently considering it to be formed of *ma*, negative, and *ik*, "wind."

It is evident, therefore, that the authorities are at sea in regard to the signification of the Maya and Tzental names. If the symbol is used, as Seler claims, to indicate offerings or sacrifices, this may be readily explained on the supposition that it is used ikonomatically because of the phonetic value I have assigned it; but otherwise it is difficult, if not impossible, to see any relation between the symbol and the name given it. So far I have found it used in no place, in combination, where the value *manik* will give a satisfactory interpretation.

The following additional renderings are added here as tending to confirm the phonetic value assigned the *manik* character.

The character shown in plate LXVIII, 37, is from Tro. 20*c, where it is repeated four times. The figures below the text show women in the act of sprinkling or pouring water on children. Whether this be considered a religious ceremony or not, it is probably intended to denote purifying or cleansing, and not baptism in the modern acceptation of the term. As *chosk*, according to Perez, signifies "to cleanse, purify, scour," and *choick* "to clean, scour, or wash the face," we have therein a quite appropriate interpretation of the symbol. The presence of the cardinal-point symbols renders it probable that the scene refers to a religious ceremony of some kind. The strict regard paid to the position relative to the cardinal points by savage and semicivilized people is too well known to require any proof here.

On Tro. 34*c two individuals are engaged in some work which we might suppose to be weaving but for the fact that there is no cord or

thread to be seen. Over each is the character shown in plate LXVIII,
38. This is evidently an incomplete *maxik* symbol. As the supposed
aspirate sign is present, it is probable that *hooch*, "to pare off, to
scrape," or *hoochei*, "to pare off, or scrape the henequin," will furnish
an appropriate rendering.

THE EIGHTH DAY

Maya, *lamat*; Tzental, *lambat*; Quiche-Cakchiquel, *canel or kanel*; Zapotec, *lapa or
laba*; Nahuatl, *tochtli*.

The various forms of the symbol of this day are shown in plates LXV,
33 to 37, and LXVIII, 39–40. That given by Landa is seen in LXV, 33;
it is also found very frequently in the codices as LXV, 34. The three
other forms found in the codices are shown in LXV, 35, 36, 37. The form
on the Palenque Tablet is given in LXVIII, 40; that of the Tikal inscription is similar to Landa's figure, if we are correct in our determination,
of which there is some doubt, as the dots are effaced.

A comparison of plate LXV, 36, with the symbol of the day *Ahau*, shown
in LXVIII, 5, leads at once to the impression that the former was derived
from the latter, and that, if in any sense phonetic, the equivalents of the
two are closely related. As will be shown hereafter, the *Ahau* symbol
has *l* as its chief phonetic element, if it be considered in any sense phonetic. We should therefore expect to find, in the verbal equivalent of
this *Lamat* symbol, *l* as a prominent element. In the form shown at
LXV, 33, it would seem that we see an effort to intimate by the character
itself the presence of the *b* element. That the symbol shown in plate
LXV, 38, has *b* as its chief element is shown elsewhere. It is possible,
therefore, that this *Lamat* symbol had no original signification purely its
own, but that it is a composite derived from the *Ahau*, and what I have
termed the *b* symbol. Without anticipating the proof that the *Ahau*
symbol has *l* as its chief phonetic element, I call attention to the fact
that it is the upper character in the symbol for *likin*, "east" (plate
LXVIII, 12). As the lower character is the well-known symbol for *kin*,
"day" or "sun," we must assume that the value of our *Ahau*, in this
case at least, is *li*. As another suggestion, I would add that it may
have been derived from a figure used in some game. As the figure is
usually divided into apartments or cells, most of which inclose a dot,
the Maya word *lom*, *lomah*, "meter, encajar, poner dentro, introducir"
(Perez), would not inappropriately express the idea. Its use as a day
symbol would then be simply for its phonetic value. This is based, of
course, on the derivation I suggest below. Nevertheless it must be
admitted that these are but mere guesses.

In his article so frequently referred to Dr Seler has little to say in
regard to the signification of the names of this day. He remarks that
"the word *kanel* is given by Ximenes—with what authority I know
not—with the signification 'rabbit,' thus corresponding to the Mexican
name for this character (Tochtli)." He says he is unable to interpret
the words *lambat* and *lamat*. In his subsequent article he interprets

the Zapotec word by "to divide, to break into pieces," and remarks "that the concept of something divided, broken in pieces, lies at the foundation of the delineation of this day character is also proved by the Maya hieroglyph for the same [see plate LXV, 33 and 36], in which something divided or broken up is undoubtedly indicated." He adds that "perhaps also the terms *lambat* and *lawat*, used in Tzental-Zoztzil and in Maya for the day character, and which are hardly explainable from the well-known Maya, are derived from the Zapotec word *lapa*."

Dr Brinton's explanation is as follows:

The Maya *lamat* is evidently a shortened form of the Tzental *lambat*, which is composed of *lam*, to sink into something soft ("hundirse in cosa blanda," like light loam), and *bat*, the grain, the seed, and the name refers to the planting of the crops. The Quiche-Cakchiquel *kanel* is the name of the Guardian of the Sown Seed, probably from *kan*, yellow, referring to the yellow grains or maize. The Zapotec *lapa* or *laba* means a drop, and a crown or garland; here probably the latter, in reference to the products of the fields. The rabbit, in Nahuatl, is the symbol of ease and intoxication.

Thus, while Dr Brinton explains the name by "sinking in the mud or soil," Brasseur explains it by "sinking in the water."

It is much more likely that the Maya name is but a modification of *lamba*, which, as a verb, according to Henderson, signifies "to flash, to shine, etc;" and as a noun, according to Perez, "resplendor, brillo, relampago." I have no Tzental vocabulary at hand, but observe that in the closely allied Zoztzil, "relampaguear" is given as the equivalent of *lamlaghet*.

It is a coincidence worthy of a passing notice that in Hawaiian *lama* and *ga-lama* signify "a torch;" *ow-lama*, "to give light;" *malama*, "light from the sun or moon;" in Samoan, *lama*, "the candle-nut tree, and a torch made of the nuts;" in Tonga, *mama*, "light, a flambeau;" New Zealand, *rama*, "candle, light;" Tahaiton, *rama*, "a torch."

It is somewhat singular that Dr Brinton, after his interpretation of the Maya name of the fourth day heretofore given, should in this instance derive *kanel*—the Quiche-Cakchiquel name of this day—from *kan*, "yellow," referring to the yellow grains of maize. However, it is quite probable that the reference to the color in this explanation is correct.

The traditions of the Indians in which the rabbit is brought into relation with the sun are well known. Dr Brinton has shown in his work on "American Hero Myths" that the Rabbit or Great Hare in the Algonquian myths symbolized "light." He remarks in "The Lenape and their Legends" that—

The familiar Algonkin myth of the "Great Hare," which I have elsewhere shown to be distinctively a myth of Light, was also well known to the Delawares, and they applied to this animal, also, the appellation of the "Grandfather of the Indians." Like the fire, the hare was considered their ancestor, and in both instances the Light was meant, fire being its symbol, and the word for hare being identical with that of brightness and light.[1]

It is possible that the Mexicans selected the rabbit for this day as a known symbol of light, thus bringing it into correspondence with the signification of the day names of the other calendars. The method by which Drs Seler and Brinton try to bring the Maya and Zapotec names into harmony with the Mexican appears to me to be in the wrong direction.

It is therefore quite probable, from what has been shown, that the Maya, Tzental, and Quiche-Cakchiquel names refer to light, flame, or the lightning flash, and that the rabbit was selected because of some mythological relation it was supposed to bear to the sun, or light.[1] As this character is seldom found in combination, or used otherwise than as a day symbol, it is probable that the signification is represented by some other symbol, or is not referred to in the text.

THE NINTH DAY

Maya, *muluc*; Tzental, *molo* or *mulu*; Quiche-Cakchiquel, *toh*; Zapotec, *niza* or *queza*; Nahuatl, *atl*.

There are but few and slight variations in the form of the symbol of this day. That given by Landa is shown in plate LXV, 39. The usual forms in the codices are seen at 40–42 of the same plate. Symbol 43, which is an important variation, is from the Cortesian Codex.

The addition of the little circle and loop in example LXV, 43, from the Cortesian Codex, is important, as it possibly indicates that the simple forms given in plate LXV, 40–42, are incomplete, and may be a slight indication of phoneticism. If the latter supposition be correct, it is probable that in this additional feature we find the element 'c of the word. It is one of the characteristics of the *manik* symbol, which, as heretofore shown, has, in some instances at least, *ck* as one of its phonetic elements, whether considered truly phonetic or not.

This clue, if followed up, appears to furnish an explanation of some other characters in which the little circle and loops are found. For example, the character shown in plate LXV, 44 (Dres. 2 (45)b and c), apparently refers to the act of sewing or stitching indicated by the pictures below the text. As the circle and loops form an important part of the character, it is probable that *c* or *ck* is the chief or prominent element of the word. It is possible therefore, that *chuguh*, "to sew," or some derivative thereof, would be a proper rendering. The glyph shown in plate LXV, 45, from Tro. 11*c is a duplication of LXV, 44. As the appendix, as shown elsewhere, probably has *ak, ku*, or *kul* as its phonetic equivalent, we have, as the elements of the word represented by the whole glyph (omitting the prefix), *ch'-ch'ak*. As *chuch* (*chuchuh*), Perez, and *chooch* (*choochoh*), Henderson, signify "to loosen, untie, disunite, detach," this may be the true interpretation of the symbol. The presence of the eye in a symbol appears, as a rule, to have no special

[1] Notwithstanding the definition given above, Dr Brinton suggests in his later work that the symbols of the day bear a close resemblance to some of the sun signs.

significance, as is shown by its presence sometimes in the symbols for the days *chicchan* and *oc*. It is worthy of note that Dr Seler introduces into his *manik* series the character above shown as having some relation to and being possibly a variation of that symbol. Before attempting to trace the symbol of the day in its combinations with other characters, with a view of ascertaining its original signification, reference will be made to the signification of the day names in the different calendars.

The signification of the Nahuatl word *atl* is water; the Zapotec names are also words for water. *Toxil* was the name of the principal Quiche deity, and appears to have been the god of thunder and rain, and, as Seler presumes, was the representative in these nations of the Maya Chac and Mexican Tlaloc. According to Brasseur, *toh* signifies "a heavy or sudden shower" or "thunder shower." Drs Seler and Brinton both derive the Maya and Tzental names from the radical *mol* or *mol*, "to join together, collect, heap up," and suppose it refers to the gathering together of the waters (that is, the clouds) in the heavens. This brings the signification of these two names into harmony with that of the names of the other calendars, and is probably a correct interpretation.

There are but few places where the symbol of this day is found in connection with other characters that I have been able to interpret entirely satisfactorily.

The compound character shown in plate LXV, 46, is from Dres. 10c. Judging by the evident parallelism of the groups in this division, this character is the symbol of the bird figured below the text. In this picture is easily recognized the head of the parrot. As *moo* is the Maya name of a species of parrot ("the macaw"), and the circular character of the glyph is like the symbol for *uaklu*, except that the circumscribing line is of dots, we may safely accept this term as the phonetic value. The fact that the small character is double, as is the *o* in the word, is another indication that the rendering is correct, and probably accounts for the circle being of dots. (See above under *akbal*.) This interpretation appears to be further supported by the form of the symbol for the month *Mol* as found at Dres. 47c. (See plate LXIV, 50.)

The hint furnished by these characters may enable us to gain a correct idea of the signification of the dotted line which surrounds one of the characters in each group of Dres. 7c, one of which is shown in plate LXV, 47. As the inclosing line of dots appears in some cases (but not all, for in some instances *o* or *u* appears to form the chief phonetic element) to indicate *uo* or *uu*, it is possible that this glyph may be properly interpreted by *uaktal*, "a gift, dower, present," or "to present a gift or dower, to offer a present." Hence the whole character shown in plate LXV, 47, may be interpreted "to make a gift of cacao."[1]

---

[1] For explanation of the twisted comb-like characters, Landa's *ca*, see Sixth Annual Report of the Bureau of Ethnology, page 255.

The usual form of the Mexican symbol of this day is shown in plate LXV, 48, the leaf-like portion being blue in the original to indicate water. In regard to the origin of the character, Seler remarks: "If the Maya character agrees with the Mexican (atl), we must look upon it as a water vessel." Yet after a number of illustrations and references he declares: "I by no means affirm that the vessel is expressed by the form of this character. The form seems to me to express rather the water drop."

It is more likely that it represents a little circular hillock, seen from above, or something of that nature surrounded by a ring, as the significations given the Maya word mul are "hillock, heap, mound, mountain, ants' nest, etc." However, if Henderson is correct in giving as one of its special meanings "one of many one," its origin may readily be seen. That it was taken from some object which could be designated by the word mul or mol may confidently be assumed. Hence the symbol is used for its phonetic value as a day character and not with any reference to the object represented. The little circle and loops seen in plate LXV, 49, from the Cortesian Codex 30b, are probably, as heretofore stated, introduced to give the c sound. Dr Brinton suggests that it represents one thing in another of the same kind, with a reference to collecting together or heaping up.

THE TENTH DAY

Maya, oc; Tzental, elab; Quiche-Cakchiquel, tzi; Zapotec, tella; Nahuatl, itzcuintli.

The symbol of this day as given by Landa is shown in plate LXV, 49. This is substantially the usual form found in the codices as given in LXV, 50, 51, 55, the first two being usual in the Troano, Cortesian, and Peresian codices, and 55 in the Dresden. In a few instances, as Tro. 12a and 12c, it assumes the face form 52. The face form shown at 54 occurs in the Dresden Codex, as do the variations seen at 53 and 56.

Dr Seler and Brasseur contend that the forms shown in plate LXV, 52 and 54, make it evident that the broken line, which is the chief characteristic of the glyph, is intended to represent, or rather is derived from, the ear of the dog. This, Seler says, is frequently represented in the Mexican codices, and also many times in the Maya manuscripts, with the tip of the ear torn away. To illustrate this, he presents several figures of dog's heads, one of which is shown in our plate LXV, 57.[1]

There would seem to be some foundation for this supposition, yet there are difficulties in the way of its acceptance which appear unsurmountable. The first of these is that it furnishes no explanation or clue to the relation between the symbol and the Maya or Tzental noun. Second, it does not appear to have been used in any instance as the symbol of the dog, which seems to be a fatal objection, if it is assumed to be merely ideographic. Third, it renders only more difficult any explanation of the character shown in plate LXV, 58, which is of such

[1] Brinton thinks that in some of the forms is indicated "a trail" or "footprints," which are meanings of oc.

frequent occurrence in all the codices. If a satisfactory interpretation of this glyph could be found, it would assist greatly in deciphering the codices. I am rather inclined to think it is a sign of repetition—as "repeat thrice." If there were some word for *ear* which could be connected with *oc* or *elub*, then we might suppose the symbol to be used phonetically. However, as this can not be found, some other explanation must be sought.

The Nahuatl and Quiche-Cakchiquel names are the ordinary terms in these languages for "dog," and the Mexican symbol for the day is the head of a dog. Dr Seler does not attempt to explain the Tzental name, and merely suggests that the Maya word *oc*, "foot, footprint, track," and as a verb, "to enter, to go into," may have been adopted by the priests as expressing a prominent characteristic of the dog. Dr Brinton is inclined to derive the name *oc* from the verb *ocol, oclah*, "to steal, to rob," rather than from *ocol*, "to enter," supposing it to have been selected as indicative of another characteristic of the dog. This he believes also to be the signification of the Tzental term *elub*. This it seems to me is again reversing the order, unless we assume that the Quiche *tzi* and Mexican *itzcuintli* are the older terms.[1]

Dr Brinton says that according to Bartolomé de Pisa the Zapotec name signifies "dog," though he does not find it with this meaning in the vocabularies. Dr Seler, however, obtains the signification "dog" for this name by supposing that it is derived from *tee-lao*, "month downward," referring to some myth of a dog representing the lightning, or lightning demon, as falling or plunging downward from the sky in certain figures of the codices. This, Dr Brinton says, "seems strained," which may also be said of the explanations of the Maya name.

The symbol of the dog as found in the Dresden Codex (13c), and as admitted by Dr Seler, is shown in plate LXV, 59. The same symbol is found in the same codex, 21b. Now, I think it possible to show, with a considerable degree of certainty, what is the chief phonetic element of this symbol, at least of its first or left-hand character. In plate LXV, 60, from Tro. 22*a, is seen (omitting the prefix) substantially the symbol that Landa interprets *le*, "the lasso," and also "to lasso." As the lower character is his *e*, we may take for granted that the upper portion indicates the *l* sound; further evidence of this, however, will be presented under the twentieth day. As this is followed by the symbol seen in plate LXV, 61, which refers to the "turkey" (kutz or cutz),[2] and the figure below the text shows a snared turkey, the interpretation appears to be appropriate. Turning now to Dres. 44 (1)c, we notice in the picture below the text the compound glyph shown in plate LXV, 62.

[1] "I was not aware that it had the signification "dog" in any of the Mayan languages, nor do I find that Seler or Brinton appeal to this fact in their efforts to explain the day name in the Maya calendar. However, Dr Brinton remarks that Brasseur and Seler think that some forms of the symbol "portray the ears of a dog, as in some of the Mayan dialects the dog is called *oc*."

[2] Dr Brinton (Primer, p. 36) says that this is called "an article of food, by Thomas." While this is correct in the same that I speak of the turkey (kutz or cutz) as food, it is incorrect in giving the impression that I interpret the symbol by "article of food," as I have always interpreted it "turkey."

Immediately below it is the figure of a fish, which the two individuals represented are trying to catch in a seine. As this contains the same elements as 61 (plate LXV), reversed, the phonetic value should be *tzc.* Referring to Perez' Lexicon, we find that *tzcc* is a fish "so named;" Brasseur says, " a little fish resembling a sardine which inhabits the *zonotes.*"

Now these give *tz* as the chief phonetic element of the left character of the dog symbol (LXV, 59), which is also the consonant element of the name for "dog" (*tzi*) in the Tzental, Cakchiquel, and most of the Maya dialects, though not of the Maya proper. This furnishes a consistent and appropriate rendering of the left portion of the symbol. Although the symbol for the month *Xaakin* (LXV, 63) presents a difficulty, it is possible some other name was applied to this month of which *tz* was a leading element; Yaxkin is sometimes written with the prefix *Dzc.*

As *och* is the Maya name for the "unic fox," and *oquil* or *ocquil* is the name in Tzental and Tzotzil for "wolf," it is possible the Maya name may have been derived from one of these. Moreover, it is worthy of notice that "foot" in Tzotzil is written *oquil* as well as *oc.*

I was at first inclined to adopt Dr Seler's suggestion that the distinguishing feature of the symbol might have been taken from the dog's ears as given in the codices. However, a more thorough examination leads me to doubt this suggestion. The little black dots or blocks on the bent line appear here, as in the *chicchan* symbol, to be the most prominent and essential elements of the symbol. As they do not appear in the ear figures, it seems impossible that the character should have been derived from these figures. It is more likely that they represent the knots on a string or cord; and this supposition appears to be sustained by the fact that the Maya word *kok,* according to Brasseur, signifies "a knot, hook;" and *kokal* "to be knotted, formed of knots." Perez says "*kok,* el lazo formado para annlar;" "*kokol,* lazarse para annlarse la cuerda." If this supposition be correct, the symbol is used for the day because of its phonetic value, and without any reference to its original signification.

THE ELEVENTH DAY

Maya, chuen: Tzental, batz: Quiche-Cakchiquel, batz: Zapotec, loo: Nahuatl, ozomatli.

The symbol of this day is subject to few and slight variations. The form given by Landa, which is also quite common in most of the codices, especially Tro. and Cort., is shown in plate LXV, 64. Slight variants are shown in LXV, 65, 66, and 67. An exceptional and peculiar form from Dres. 32b is seen in LXV, 68. A form from the Perez codex in which an eye is introduced is given at LXV, 69. The character on the Palenque Tablet and some other inscriptions, which is supposed to be the symbol of this day, is shown at LXV, 70, but the proof that it is, in those cases, the day symbol is not so conclusive as that in regard to

other day symbols, as no method of bringing it into relation with the
other time symbols of the inscriptions has been found.

A closely corresponding form is seen in the symbol for the month Tzec
as found in the Dres. Codex (see plate LXV, 71). If the glyphs are in any
sense phonetic, it is probable that in the comb-like appendage to this
symbol (Landa's cu) we have the 'c (k) sound, and that the variation in
the main character from the usual ahau glyph (in having the bounding
line open and turned right and left at the top) is indicative of the
variation in the phonetic value. The explanation of the symbol, which
replaces the eye in the dog or panther like figure in Tro. 32c and 33c, and
is alluded to by Dr Seler in this connection (LXVI, 1), has already been
given under the discussion of the "Third Day." There, as I have
shown, it probably indicates the Maya word chac, "heat, warmth,"
alluding to the hot, dry season which parches and shrivels up the growing corn. This explanation retains the phonetic value of the symbol,
and it appears also to be entirely consistent with the figures found in
connection with it.

There is another symbol closely allied in form (plate LXVI, 2) which
is of frequent occurrence in the codices, usually, and, in fact, almost
exclusively, in the picture spaces, and apparently bearing some relation
to the offerings. It is often in groups, and is many times repeated in
groups on the so-called "title pages" of the Tro. and Cort. manuscripts.
It, however, frequently occurs in the form seen in the dog's eye (LXVI, 1),
grouped as the other (Dres., 26a, etc) and undoubtedly used as an
equivalent, as we find numerals attached as with the other form. The
only distinction, as will be observed, is the presence or absence of the
little divided square at the top. As that with the divided square is
more detailed, it is probably the correct form, and, if so, can not be
distinguished from the Ahau symbol.

On Dres. 29b, 30b, and 31b the symbol shown in plate LXVI, 3, is found
in each group of characters. This bears a close resemblance to the symbol
for the month Tzec, but varies in some important respects, as will be seen
by comparison. The appendix, as I am inclined to believe, gives the
ah, ka, or kal sound, and shows that it is a verb or word indicating
action. As we find in each group the figure or symbol of a food animal, the whole series may be supposed to relate to feasts, or eating, or
the collection of food. This suggestion is strengthened by the fact that
the kan or maize symbol is placed in connection with the animal figures.
It is possible, therefore, that this character may be correctly rendered
by tziclin (tziclintah), "to distribute, share, divide among many." As
it is followed in each case by a cardinal-point symbol, and the symbol
of the double tusgned or toothed deity, probably Itzamna, is found in
each group, it is probable that the text relates to religious festivals.
This interpretation, however, is a mere suggestion or guess, which as
yet I am unable to fortify by any other evidence than the resemblance
of the main character to the Tzec symbol.

COPIES OF GLYPHS FROM THE CODICES

The Nahuatl, Tzental, and Quiche-Cakchiquel names of this day are the ordinary terms in these languages for "monkey." Dr Brinton thinks the Maya name, which does not appear to have any signification in this language as a separate word (though *chuench* is "aborous, tuble," "a certain tree"), is derived from a Tzental term, *chix*, which is applied to a particular species of monkey. He and Dr Seler refer to the *chuen* in a legend of the Popol Vuh, which undoubtedly stands in close relation to *batz* or "monkey," there spoken of as *hunbatz*. As these words in the Quiche myth appear unquestionably to refer to a species of the monkey tribe, or mythical persons under the symbolism of monkeys, the conclusion they reach is probably correct, and justifies the belief that the Maya name should be interpreted "monkey."

The origin of the symbol is uncertain, and Dr Seler makes no attempt to explain it. The difference between the simple form with the three teeth only (plate LXVI, 2) and the typical *Chuen* symbol indicates a difference in the word equivalents, or in the signification if ideographic. It is possible that Brasseur is right in rendering the former by *co*, which signifies "tooth;" in which case we may be justified in assuming that the additions in the *Chuen* symbol give the additional phonetic elements in the word. It may be, as supposed by some authors, that it was intended to represent the front view of an open mouth of some animal, as *chi* is the Maya word for mouth.

THE TWELFTH DAY

Maya. *eb*; Tzental. *enob*; Quiche-Cakchiquel. *e* or *ee*; Zapotec. *pija*; Nahuatl. *ozomatli or itzcuintli*.

There are comparatively few variations in the symbol of this day; some, however, are of sufficient importance to render recognition doubtful but for their presence in the day series. That given by Landa is seen in plate LXVI, 4; the form most usual in the Tro. and Cort. codices is that shown in LXVI, 5; the variations seen in LXVI, 6, 7, 8, are from the Dresden Codex, and that in LXVI, 9, is from the Peresianus.

This character occurs very seldom, if ever, except as a day symbol, hence it is presumed to be purely ideographic or pictorial. There is, however, a deity symbol found in the Tro. Codex (plate LXVI, 10) in which we see apparently the chief characteristic of the *eb* symbol. Here, however, instead of a dot-bordered tooth, there is a dot-bordered dark stripe which runs downward entirely across the face. This is accompanied usually by the numeral prefix 11. The symbol of the same deity as found in the Dresden Codex is shown in plate LXVI, 11. Here the stripe is reduced to a single broken line. Dr Schellhas contends that he is a Death god and the equivalent of the Mexican Xipe. That he is a god of the underworld in the Tro. Codex is apparent from his ornaments and the dotted lines on his body or limbs; yet in two instances— plates 5 a and b—he is represented as a traveling merchant. Whether the deity in the Dresden Codex is the same as that of the Tro. Codex is not positively certain, but the presence of the numeral 11 with the symbol, and in some instances the dotted lines on the body of the deity, indicate that the two are identical. Whether this deity glyph bears any relation to the day symbol is, however, doubtful. The only names of Maya deities I find with *buluc* ("eleven") as a prefix are Ahbuluc Ilnaxx and Buluc-Ahau (?). The first, which signifies "He of the Eleven Tigers," was one of the idols made at the festival of the new year Canac. On one of the four plates of the Dresden Codex representing the festivals of the new year (36a) we observe that the image carried by the chac is a tiger-like animal marked with dotted lines. Whether this is to be connected with the deity above mentioned is doubtful. The other name, Buluc-Ahau, mentioned by Landa, is the name of one of the signs of the Katun given in his figure of the cycle, and, although he names the word "idol," does not appear to refer to any particular deity.

In regard to the names of the first three calendars, Dr Seler remarks as follows:

E, ye signifies "the edge," "sharpness," "the notch;" *eb, chil, chal, yebul*, "a row of notches," "flight of steps," "stairs." In Quiche-Cakchiquel *e* signifies "the tooth." "the edge;" *ee* is the plural form in Cakchiquel of the word, as *eeb* of the Quiche; *eeb* is a born plural form in the Tzental, as I think, from a singular *eeer*. The name must denote the same thing in all the languages, i. e., "a row of teeth," "flight of steps"—a signification which harmonizes excellently with many Mexican forms of the character (plate LXVI, 13) as well as with the Maxtlan name of it (idem, "his tooth").

Dr Brinton says that "in Maya *eb* is the plural of *e*, which means 'points' or 'ends,' like those of pins or thorns, and plainly was intended to designate the broom by reference to its numerous points. From the same idea, rows of teeth received the same name. The Tzental and Quiche names *e* and *eeb*—the latter a plural—were from the same radical and had the same signification." He says the Nahuatl and Zapotec names both signify the brush or broom of twisted twigs, or stiff grass used for cleaning and dusting, and also this grass itself. Thus he brings the names of the five calendars into harmony. This explanation corresponds with that given by Clavigero of the Mexican term, which he says is the name of a certain plant of which brooms were made.

I am inclined to believe the symbol in this instance is a mere pictograph intended to represent the tip of some lanceolate leaf, the dots denoting the hairs along the edge. The tips of the "reed grass," as shown in the symbolic representation of *Zacatla* ("Nombres Geográficos" by Peñafiel; plate LXVI, 13), would give precisely the dot-bordered tooth in the symbol. It is to be observed, however, that the Mexican symbol for this day, the usual form of which is shown in LXVI, 14, is essentially different and has joined with the green blades the skeleton underjaw. In some instances, as at *Malinaltepec* ("Nombres Geográficos"), the entire skull is added. A more elaborate form of the symbol, from the Borgian Codex plate 20, is given in LXVI, 15. Here the skeleton jaw is replaced by the roots of the plant; observe, however, the brush-like projections above. Are we to see in this associated death's-head a reference to death, or rather to the earth, a symbolism undoubtedly found in the Tro. Codex? Or must we suppose that behind the name is to be found the signification of the Mextitlan name *tlan*, from *tlantli*, "tooth?" Dr Seler remarks that "it seems to me quite possible that the point surrounded by dots in the character *eb* is an abbreviation of figure 326" (the prefix to our plate LXIV, 48).[1]

THE THIRTEENTH DAY

Maya, *ben* or *been*; Tzental, *ben*; Quiche-Cakchiquel, *ah*; Zapotec, *quii, ii*, or *laa*; Nahuatl, *acatl*.

The symbol of this day is subject to but few and, with one or two exceptions, but slight variations. Landa's figure is represented at LXVI, 16, those usual in the codices in LXVI, 17. 18. 19, and an irregular form found in Dres. 10c in symbol 20 of the same plate. When used in combination with other glyphs and otherwise than as a day symbol, the form, though usually typical, is subject occasionally to wide variations, though there is considerable doubt whether the latter are to be considered *ben* symbols.

Dr Seler contends that the figure originated from the plaited reed or mat, which, if correct, enables us to trace it by gradations to a wholly different figure. But before referring further to these, it is best that the signification of the names should be given as determined by linguistic evidence.

The Nahuatl name *acatl* signifies "reed," "cane," or "stalk;" and, according to Ximenes and Brasseur, the Quiche-Cakchiquel *ah* also signifies "reed," especially the "cornstalk" or "sugar cane." The Zapotec *quii* has also the same signification, "reed," and Dr Brinton says *laa* has the same meaning, but Dr Seler says he can not find it with this signification in the lexicons, nor do I find it in any to which I have access. The Maya and Tzental *ben*, however, presents a more serious difficulty in the attempt to bring it into harmony with the others. Dr Seler contents himself with reference to certain words which have *ben* or *bex* as their root. This root, he says, signifies "consumed," and the words to which he refers mean "to be consumed," "to waste away," "to fail, be lacking, go away." This is also the signification to which Dr Brinton refers. "I find," he says, "that in Tzental the dried corn-stalk (*caña de maiz seco*) is called *cogh-bex*, and from this I doubt not this day-name in that dialect and the Maya was taken and syncopated. The verb *ben* or *bex* in Tzental means 'to walk, to go,' but in the above compound the *bex* is from the Maya stem *benel*, 'to be used up, to be dead.'"

The opinion of Dr Seler, above stated, that the symbol of this day originated from the delineation of the plaited reed or mat, is based on

---
[1] Dr Brinton says it is the face of an old woman with a peculiar painted earmark.

the representation of the mat both in symbols and figures in the Mexican and Maya codices. Some of these are shown in our plate LXVI, 21 to 24. The first, 21, is from the Mendoza Codex, and is found also in Tro. 20*d. These are undoubtedly intended to denote mats or something of a kindred nature. The same figure is seen on the roofs of temples and houses, one of which is shown in LXVI, 22, from Tro. 10*c. In these instances they appear to indicate the thatching with which the roof is covered. The form is sometimes varied, as in LXVI, 23, from Tro. 10*a. The symbol which, it is presumed, refers to the mat as seen in Tro. 21*d. is given in LXVI, 24; that representing the house in Tro. 10*e is seen in LXVI, 25; another of a slightly different form, from Tro. 7*c, in LXVI, 26; and another, referring also to a house or to the roof, as Dr Seler supposes, is given in LXVI, 27.

There can be no question that plate LXVI, 21, is intended to represent a mat or something of that nature, nor that the character shown at 24 is the symbol used to represent this mat, straw, or plaited fabric; nor can it be doubted that the figures shown at 22 and 23 are conventional figures for houses of some kind. It must also be admitted that the characters shown at 25, 26, and 27 are symbols denoting these houses. According to Dr Seler's interpretation, figures 24 and 27 are, in some cases, used "to denote a seat on a mat [24]; sometimes the mat roof of the temple or the temple itself" (27). In his opinion these characters, especially 27, contain "the element of the mat and a symbol of carrying—the hand or elements which have been borrowed from the figure of the hand—and in these hieroglyphs the transition of the realistically delineated mat into the character *ben* may be distinctly traced."

That the upper part of plate LXVI, 25 and 26, and of other similar figures in the codices which might be shown, do make a close approach in form to the *ben* symbol, must be admitted. But there is one break in the chain which needs to be closed before the evidence is entirely satisfactory. Does the upper part of these house symbols (25-26) indicate roof mats or thatching? An examination of the house figures shows these supposed mat figures to be something standing on the top of the roof—something rising, as it were, perpendicularly along and above the comb or crest. Now, precisely such battlements or elevated crests appear to have been common on the roofs of the temples or structures which have been preserved to modern times. We see them in the figures given by Charnay, Stevens, and other explorers; and what is worthy of special notice in this connection is, that they sometimes consist of openwork or trellis-like figures. Therefore, if we connect the upper part of the house symbols with the *ben* glyph, it is still by no means certain that it is derived from, or bears any relation to, the mat character. We notice farther that in the figures of houses this supposed mat figure is not used to indicate the thatching, but is clearly distinguished from it. Again, if the upper characters of LXVI, 25, 26, are intended to signify the thatching, roof matting, or roof, and are simple ideograms drawn from the thing represented, then the lower characters in these symbols might well be supposed to represent the wall or framework of the house. But the widely different relations in which we find this lower character forbid this conclusion. That the wall may be indicated is true, but if so it must be ikonomatically or by the phonetic value of the symbol. I have therefore found it very difficult to reach any entirely satisfactory conclusion in regard to these house symbols. That the lower character is phonetic in the true or rebus sense can, I think, be shown, but, notwithstanding the objections I have presented, the most satisfactory interpretation of the upper part is that it represents the roof, as we see in the upper figure of LXVI, 25, the crosshatching and the double bee lines. Hence it would seem satisfactory to consider it merely an ideogram or picture but for the prefix, which can not be readily accounted for on the idea of a pictorial representation.

As we have found that the lower character of plate LXVI, 26, has the phonetic value of *ek* usually combined with *o* or *a* (see remarks above on LXV, 41), we may find in this glyph *otoch*, "house," though the full signification of the entire compound symbol appears to embrace more than this. Possibly the upper part is a determinative. The lower part, however, of LXVI, 26 and 27, is found, as before remarked, where it can have no reference to a building. As it has the two heavy lines indicative of the *p* sound (see explanation of LXIV, 11), and also of the guttural, it is probable that the signification, where a structure is referred to, is *pak* (*pakal*), "a building, wall, fortification." But when it is found in an entirely different relation, as in Tro. 17b, where it is over an individual tying a deer, it must have an entirely different signification. It is possible that it may be consistently rendered by *paue* (*paauah*), "to cord, fasten, bind" (Henderson), or some derivative thereof. We find it again on Tro. 10*d and 20*d, and Dres. 18c, Le, and 20c, where females are represented as bearing burdens on their backs. Now, *cuch* signifies "to bear, to carry," and also "a load, a burden," and *cuch-pach*, "a carrier, a porter" (literally "to carry on the back," *pach* denoting "back").

In this instance also the phonetic value assigned it holds good. On Tro. 17b the same glyph stands above an individual who is in the act of striking a snake which is biting his foot. In this case it has a suffix like that to LXVI, 3, which, as we have stated, probably represents the sound *ak, ka,* or *kal,* and indicates that the word is a verb. There are several words containing the phonetic value assigned the character, which are applicable, as *pakchetah,* which Perez interprets "pisar, poner el pie sobre algo;" *packah,* "despachurran, machucar;" *puchuk,* "to scatter, break" (H.); *pch,* "to crush" (H.); *paez* (*paeah*), "to squeeze, press, crush" (H.).

It seems, therefore, quite probable that the lower part of these compound symbols is phonetic.

If Dr Seler is correct in his supposition that the symbol is derived from the plaited mat, then it is most likely simply ideographic or a mere conventional pictograph. Possibly this is the correct conclusion, as I can find no evidence tending to show that it is phonetic. If we could suppose the form was intended to represent a "road" or "pathway"—*be, beil,* and *bel* in Maya, and *beel* in Zotzil—we might assume it to be phonetic.

The combinations shown in plate LXVI, 28, 29, 30, and 55, in which the symbol of this day appears, have as yet received no satisfactory explanation. Those shown in LXVI, 28, and 55, are of very frequent occurrence and probably indicate some common ceremony, order, or direction in the religious ceremonies. I have a strong suspicion that the first indicates exorcism or driving away the evil spirits, but I find no appropriate Maya word unless it be *pokokabil,* given by Henderson. This, however, does not agree with the interpretation *Xintchkekmo,* given by Seler to LXVI, 29, above referred to. Seler gives to LXVI, 30, the apparently strained interpretation, "he who is conquered in war and brought home prisoner." I have no interpretation to offer.[1]

THE FOURTEENTH DAY

Maya, *ix* or *hix;* Tzental, *hix;* Quiche-Cakchiquel, *balam, giz,* or *hiz;* Zapotec, *eche;* Nahuatl, *ocelot.*

The symbol of this day is found in quite a number of different forms, some of which are wide variations from the prevailing type.

Landa's figure is shown in plate LXVI, 31. The usual forms found in the Tro. Codex are LXVI, 32 to 37; 36 is somewhat rare. That shown at 38 is found only on plate 30*c, and that showing the animal head (39) on plate 12c. No essential variations from these are found in either the Codex Peresianus or Cortesianus. Those shown in LXVI, 40-42, are from the Dresden Codex.

The Nahuatl name and the Quiche-Cakchiquel, *balam,* denote the "tiger," possibly the jaguar, though the Mexican name certainly refers to the *ocelot.* Dr Brinton says that the Zapotec *eche,* or in the full form *be-eche-gala,* has the same signification. Dr Seler, however, derives it from the term *poche-tao,* "the great animal"—the tiger, or ferocious animal. But the other names, *ix, hix, hiix* or *giz,* as they are variously written (though really one word), present a more serious difficulty to the attempt to bring them into harmony with the others.

Dr Seler says:

The Cakchiquel term *giz,* i. e., the Maya *h-ex,* "the sorcerer," may well be considered as giving an explanation of the Maya name of this day character (*ix*). My conception, after one more link in the chain of evidence pointing toward it, is that the day-character system has become known to the Mayas through the medium of the cognate branches of Chiapas, for we frequently find the Tzental-Zotzil *x* corresponding to the Maya *x.*

---

[1] Brinton says the bit symbol looks to him "like a wooden bridge, the two supports of which are shown and which was sometimes covered with a straw mat." If so, it must be shown in profile, and the hanging marks above (see LXVI. 12. 17, 18) would seem to be without signification; moreover, in LXVI, 12, the supports hang from above, which would, on this theory, imply a hanging bridge.

Dr Brinton says that the Maya, Tzental, and Cakchiquel word *hiz* or *iz* means "sorcerer," though he does not furnish the evidence. Moreover, he adds immediately after that "it is probable *iz* is a variant of *ik* or *igk* 'wind, breath, life,'" and makes the connection by referring to the fact that blowing was practised in medicine rites. It would have been more satisfactory, however, had he given the evidence on which he based his assertion that the Maya and Tzental name means "sorcerer." According to Ximenes the Cakchiquel name *yiz* denotes the "sorcerer;" and it is probable that the signification of *iz* or *hiz* is the same, as the codices appear to give support to this conclusion.

On Dres. 8a the character shown in plate LXVI, 43, stands in the text over the figure of a tiger, and evidently refers to it. The close resemblance of this to the *iz* symbol from Tro. 12c shown in LXVI, 30, is too manifest to be overlooked. The same symbol is found in Tro. 17c, but here the prefix is changed to the numeral 4; below is a tiger-like animal with a feathered tongue protruding from its mouth. I have taken for granted, from the indicated action and my interpretation of one of the accompanying symbols, that this figure was intended to indicate the sorcerer or diviner. This supposition I admit is not supported by sufficient evidence to demand acceptance. However, it is probable that Léon de Rosny is justified in rendering LXVI, 43, by *ek-balam*. This supposition will be strengthened by any evidence tending to show that the prefix is properly interpreted by *ek*.

The symbol for the month *Ceh*, as given in Dres. 49a, is shown in LXVI, 44, and is the same as Landa's figure minus the suffix or month determinative. It would seem from the fact that the lower character of this symbol is the same as the lower portion of the symbols for Tzec (LXIV, 12) and Zac (LXVI, 48), that the word *Ceh*, if the writing is phonetic or ikonomatic, does not give the entire phonetic equivalent unless the *z* or *c* of the other names is here softened to *h*. It may be added, however, that Henderson gives both *Ceh* and *Kec* as the name of the month and the Maya name for "deer." In the Zotzil vocabulary "ciervo" is *chig* and "venado" *chigh*. There is, however, a difficulty in harmonizing this with the symbol for the month *Zip*—in which the same character appears—that I have not been able to explain. Nevertheless, it may be said, as the lower character appears (from evidence that will not be introduced at this point) to have a *z* or *dz* as its chief phonetic element, that it is possible the name had sometimes *ek* or *ke* prefixed. Running through the lower division of plates 46–50 of the Dresden Codex is a line consisting of repetitions of the character shown in LXVI, 45. Here we have again our *k*, *ke*, or *ek* glyph as a prefix. The right portion of the symbol bears a somewhat close resemblance to some forms of the symbol of the day *Lamat* (but not to *kin*, as has been suggested), and is so interpreted by Brasseur and Léon de Rosny. As *ek* signifies "star," and *lembe* "resplendent, bright, shining, sparkling," the phonetic value of the glyph may be "the bright, shining star," alluding to Venus. According to Henderson, *cekil*, *ekil*, or *gekil* was used to designate this star,

castal being added to name it as a "morning star." According to the
"Report on the city of Valladolid,"[1] the name given the "morning
star" was xock ek (or equä). It is possible, therefore, that Dr Förste-
mann is right in supposing that the long numeral series running through
plates 46–50 of this codex relates to the apparent revolution of the
planet Venus.

In Dres. 18c is the compound symbol shown in plate LXVI, 46, followed by 47. In the former we see our ek or ke symbol as the upper
character and the supposed cimi (LXV, 28) glyph as the lower character,
and to the left a prefix. This prefix is precisely that in the symbol for
the month Zac (LXVI, 43), and has presumably the same value in one
glyph as the other. This will give, as the proper rendering of the symbol LXVI, 46, zeak-cimil, "the skull of the dead." By referring to the
figure below the text, a woman is seen bearing on her back a skull
inclosed in a wrapping of some kind, which in Kingsborough, where the
color is retained, appears to be cloth. This certainly agrees with the
rendering of the glyph. The symbol which follows it, shown in LXVI,
47, has one of the elements of LXVI, 27, and, as suggested under "the
Thirteenth Day," should probably be interpreted zackpack, "a carrier or
porter" (or "bear upon the back"). In the corresponding glyph in Tro.
20*d (LXVI, 24) the upper portion, as above stated, refers probably to
the hamper or basket-like holder in which the load is carried, and is a
simple ideogram; but here (LXVI, 47) the upper character is phonetic,
corresponding very closely to the lower part of the symbols for the
months Tzec and Zac. The character which follows—the lower left-
hand of the group of four—seen at LXVI, 49, is the well-known symbol
for woman. As the women were the burden bearers in Yucatan, the
interpretation appears to be consistent. It is therefore probable that
the prefix to LXVI, 48, is to be interpreted by ek, as Rosny has suggested.

Seler, alluding to the symbol, asks, "May not the skin of the tiger,
instead of the animal itself, be here indicated?" He further suggests
that it represents the round hairy ear and the spotted skin of the tiger,
and that the glyph shown at LXVI, 50, represents the entire head of
this animal, of which there can be little doubt.

Some of the symbols of this day, found in the Fejérváry Codex, one
of which is shown in LXVIII, 41, appear to favor Seler's idea.[2]

THE FIFTEENTH DAY

Maya, men: Tzontal, tziquin: Quiche-Cakchiquel, tziquin; Zapotec, xoo or laa;
Nahuatl, quauhtli.

Landa's figure is so imperfect in this case that it is not given. The
usual forms and variations are shown in plate LXVI, 50 to 54. The last
two, which show the widest variation, are from the Dresden Codex.

[1] Cong. Inter. Americanistes, 1881, tom. 2.
[2] Dr Brinton says the usual form suggests scattered grain-husks, the word for which is xiks.

The Tzental and Quiche-Cakchiquel, *tziquin*, signifies "bird" in general, and the Nahuatl, *quauhtli*, "eagle." The Maya and Zapotec names are more difficult to bring into harmony with the others. Dr Brinton thinks that the Zapotec name is derived from *na*, "to know, to understand, to be able through knowledge." This, he says, "exactly corresponds to the Maya *men*, which means to understand, to be able to do . . . : hence in this latter tongue, *ah-men* means the man of knowledge, the wise one, the master of wisdom." "The bird," he adds, "was the symbol of wisdom and knowledge."

Dr Seler says it is difficult to determine the Yucatan name. However, from the form of the symbol he concludes it is intended to represent an aged face, by which he connects it with an aged goddess, Ixchel, the companion of Itzamna, and with certain Mexican deities. In his subsequent paper he says the Zapotec name furnishes linguistic proof of the above conclusion. "I had concluded," he says, "that the Maya hieroglyph represented the image of the old earth mother, the universally worshipped goddess called Touantzin, 'our mother,' who is connected in the Codex Vienensis with the eagle symbol." He then adds that the Zapotec term *ñaa* or *ñaa* signifies "mother," and thus finds the connection between the calendar names.

It is probable we will not be far wrong if we assume that reference to the bird as used in this connection is not so much to it as an animal as an augury, sign, or portent. The birds introduced in the Dresden and Troano codices, especially those on pages 16, 17, and 18 of the former and 18* and 19* of the latter, are supposed to have reference to auguries. In the "Vocabulario Castellano Zapoteco," under "Ave," we find *mani-bitci*, "ave agorera." In the Dresden Codex (17b) one of the birds introduced as playing this rôle is an eagle, or some rapacious species resembling an eagle or vulture. Although Seler believes the symbol to have been derived from the aged wrinkled female face, yet he closes his observations on this day in his first article as follows:

> I think the reference to the eagle is very distinctly indicated [referring to a number of glyphs accompanying or indicating an eagle-like bird]. We can understand that these hieroglyphs were annexed as attributes of the deities. But how is it that figures 687–691 [same as our plate LXVIII, 12] serve as a seat for the Chac? Now Chac (he refers to the long-nose god) is not really a god of water, but of rain; the rain-producing stone cloud is his vehicle; the stone idol is his beast of burden on which he rides.

It follows from this, notwithstanding his supposition in regard to the origin of the symbol, that he looks upon it as signifying the eagle, or bird. However, the explanations given by Drs Brinton and Seler of the Maya name fail to make a satisfactory connection between the names in the different calendars.

Not only do we find birds introduced on the pages of the Troano and Dresden codices above referred to, apparently for the purpose of indicating augury, but on Dres. 60b we see the long-nose god (probably Itzamna) sitting on the glyph LXVIII, 42, holding a bird in his arms.

Also on Dres. 73b, where the groups are composed of short columns, each apparently relating to storms, winds, etc, we see in the right-hand group the bird and men-like glyph associated. Whether these are in fact men glyphs is a question not yet determined. I am as yet unable to interpret satisfactorily any of the compound characters of which these supposed men glyphs form a part. If the form shown in LXVI, 28, the lower portion of which is substantially the same as Landa's first l, is to be accepted as equivalent to LXVI, 55, then it is probable that the symbol of the day does not indicate the phonetic value of the name. This would lead to the supposition that the name men is not the original one applied to the day, or that the symbol has been changed. I am inclined to believe one or the other of these suppositions to be correct. If the symbol could be identified in the inscriptions, I would adopt the first supposition until substantial evidence of its erroneousness could be produced.

I am unable to offer any suggestions as to the origin of the symbol. I do not think the suggestion that it is intended to represent an aged face of woman or man of any force or worthy of serious consideration. The symbol would be just as complete so far as its signification is concerned without the eye as with it.

THE SIXTEENTH DAY

Maya, cib; Tzental, chabin; Quiche-Cakchiquel, ahmak; Zapotec, guiloo or loo; Nahuatl, cozcaquauhtli. In addition to these the following are also given: Pipil, tecolotl; Mextitlan, twil tioani or tecatloti.

The forms of this symbol shown in plates LXVI, 56 to 58, and LXVII, 1 to 3, are those usually found in the codices, the slight differences being due to the greater or less degree of perfection with which they have been made. Landa's figure is similar to LXVII, 1. The variants in LXVII, 4 and 5, are from Dres. 46 and 49; but the symbols found in the day columns of Dres. 46 to 50 must not be taken as evidence of peculiar types, as they are to a large extent dashed off without care, one or two of a column being sufficiently exact for determination and the rest mere blotches. I have referred to them here and under other days simply because Dr Seler has noticed them; hence had I failed to allude to them it might be thought an oversight. However, I do not think any of the variations in the day columns of these five plates should be taken into consideration as types.

The Nahuatl name cozcaquauhtli is the "royal zopilote" (sarcoramphus papa of ornithologists). Drs Seler and Brinton agree in the supposition that the Zapotec name is derived from balloo, "the raven or crow." Dr Seler says that the Quiche-Cakchiquel word ahmak seems to signify the vulture, "who pecks out the eyes," "who makes deep holes;" while Dr Brinton maintains that the Quiche ahmak means "the master of evil," referring to the owl, which is esteemed a bird of evil omen and bad fortune. The Pipil tecolotl also denotes "the night bird or owl."

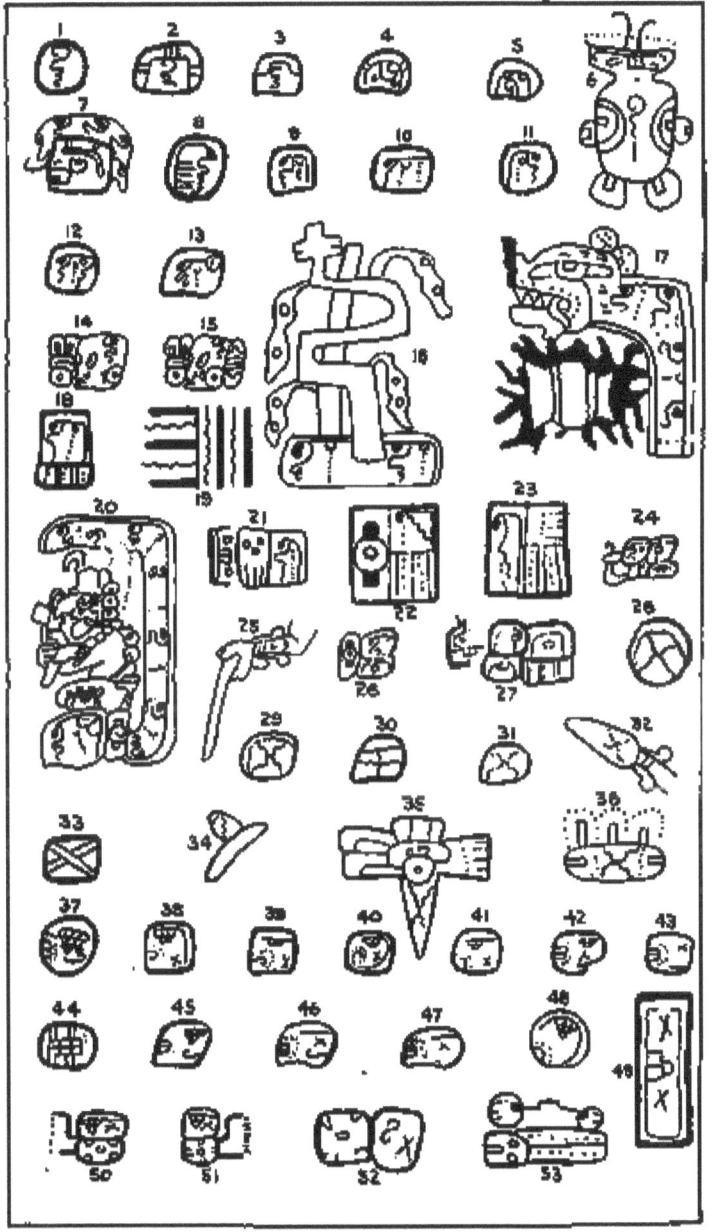

COPIES OF GLYPHS FROM THE CODICES

The Maya and Tzental names, however, present a difficulty not so easily explained. The signification of the former is "wax, gum, or copal gum," and also, according to Henderson, "root." According to Brinton the Tzental radical *chab* means "honey, wax, bee, a late meal." He refers, however, to the Cakchiquel, where he finds that *ch'ab* means "mud, clay, mire," and suggests that " as red and black clays were the primitive pigments this may connect the Tzental day name with the Maya." Seler, however, derives the Maya name from *ci* or *cii*, "to taste good," "to smell good;" and as *ci* is also the name of the maguey plant, and likewise refers to the pulque or intoxicating drink from this plant, he concludes that *cib* must have been formed by the addition of the instrumental suffix, and hence refers to that which is used for wine, "either the honey, or, more correctly, the narcotic root."

This conclusion he thinks is strengthened by the fact that the corkscrew figure, which is the chief element of the *cib* symbol, is found several times on vases or earthen vessels (see LXVII, 6). Attention is called in this connection to the fact that *loo* in Zapotec signifies "root," which is also one of the meanings given by Henderson to the Maya *cib*, which would seem to strengthen Dr Seler's conclusion.

The glyph is seldom if ever found in combination with other characters or used otherwise than as a day symbol. This, together with the fact that it is not found except as a day symbol in the beekeeper's calendar in the Troano Codex, would seem to indicate that there has been a change in the name of the day since the origin of the symbol; or, on the other hand, the symbol has been modified from some older form. Nevertheless, there are some indications that it is phonetic and that the corkscrew figure has *b* as its chief element, whether *cib* be the word indicated or not.

In the symbol for the day *Caban* (LXVII, 9) we see the same corkscrew figure, and observe that *b* is the chief consonant element of the word. In the well-known symbol for woman (LXVI, 49) there appears the same character, usually double, one at the front of the face, the other on the back part of the head. I have usually considered this a mere conventional symbol, taken from the female head, these corkscrew figures indicating the rolls of hair. Nevertheless it is possible that it is phonetic, as we see on the cheek the *c*, *ch*, or *k* character heretofore referred to. As *chap*, *chupal*, and *chuplal* are names for "woman, female, or girl," the *p* may replace the *b* and represent the corkscrew figure. I am unable, however, to explain the prefix, which should have the *b* or *p* sound, or be a determinative. Possibly it may denote *pal*, signifying a young person, though this appears to refer generally to the male sex. Henderson, however, prefixes *x* to give it the signification "daughter, or girl."

That the symbol on vessels as shown in LXVII, 6, indicates liquid, or drink of some kind, is more than probable. It may refer to *bakac* (or *balaze*), the ceremonial drink, the symbol indicating the phonetic element *b*.

The upper portion of the figure shown in LXVII, 7, from Tro. 3*b and 4*b (in the space) I was at first inclined to regard as a reptile of some kind, but the fact of its presence in the section relating to bees and honey, and the corkscrew markings, render it probable that it is beeswax. To this evidence may be added the fact that the symbol over which it is placed contains some of the elements of the *cib* glyph. There are a number of places where quite similar markings appear on seats and other things, but these are distinguished by the added line of dots, showing it, as will be seen hereafter, to be in these cases the *cab* or *caban* symbol.

The facts which have been mentioned, together with the form of the symbol, may possibly lead to a correct understanding of its origin. It seems probable that the corkscrew figure, which is the chief, and apparently only, essential element, is taken from the root of a plant and was the conventional method of representing that object. As it appears from Henderson's Lexicon that "root" was one signification of *cib* (probably from *cibak*, "to follow, succeed," which also signifies "born, manifested, root," alluding to origin), and also that in Zotzil *yib* or *yibel* is "root" (*raiz de arbol*, *yibel-te*), we find the reason why this was selected as the symbol to express the sound *cib*. The fact that in the Zapotec *loo* signifies "root" strengthens this conclusion and indicates that the symbol is not used simply for the sound indicated—that is, phonetically or ikonomatically—but also with reference to the signification.

THE SEVENTEENTH DAY

Maya, *caban*; Tzental, *chic*; Quiche-Cakchiquel, *noh*; Zapotec, *xoo*; Nahuatl, *ollin*. In addition to these, the following are also sometimes given: In Mexitlan, *naled olli*; Pipil, *tecpila nakeatl*.

This character, as is apparent from plate LXVII, 8–13, is subject to no material variation; in fact, to no variation which would prevent us from at once identifying it. That shown in LXVII, 8, is Landa's figure. The change in position of the black spot and lines with reference to one another does not appear to have any significance. In the Troano and Cortesian codices the black dot is sometimes on one side and sometimes on the other. In the Dresden Codex, however, it is nearly always on the left. The one shown in LXVII, 13, in which there is introduced a new element, is found several times in the last part of the Dresden Codex.

This character is used very frequently otherwise than as a day symbol, being found separate and in combination, also as a mark on a number of articles. As it is possible to determine with reasonable, and in fact satisfactory, certainty its signification in a number of instances where used otherwise than as a day symbol, some of these will be noticed, as they seem to furnish strong evidence of phoneticism. But I repeat here the statement made at the commencement of this paper, that in using this term "phoneticism," I include that which may, in a strict classification, be called ikonomatic. However, before referring to these, it is best to give the interpretations of the names which have been suggested, as the bearing of any interpretations of the symbols will then be better understood.

The Mexican name *ollin* or *olin* is generally interpreted "motion or movement," with special reference to the earthquake. Dr Seler, however, adds "caoutchouc ball." In his first paper, heretofore referred to, he remarks in regard to the Maya, Tzental, and Quiche-Cakchiquel names: "There is not much to be drawn from these words." In his subsequent paper he apparently relies upon the usual signification of the Mexican term, and from this and the signification of the Zapotec *xoo*, "powerful, strong, violent," concludes that the Tzental name may be consistently rendered by "large, powerful," and the Maya name by "that which is brought down, which is above," reference being made to ascending and descending. Dr Brinton derives the Maya term from *cab*, "might or strength," on the authority of the *Motul Dicc.*, and says that in this sense it corresponds precisely with the Tzental *chic* (equal Maya *chich*, "cosa fuerte y dura"), the Quiche-Cakchiquel *ah*, "strong, great," and the Zapotec *xoo*, "force, power, or might." Dr Seler, however, concludes that the Zapotec name is here to be interpreted "earth," or to be understood as referring to the earth. He thinks that the day symbol is an abbreviated form of, or derived from, LXVI, 49, which he takes to be a symbol of the goddess Chichina or Ixchebelyax, whom he identifies with Xmucu, "the white maiden." As will be observed, we have expressed the opinion that this glyph is a symbol for woman in the general sense, which conclusion appears to be confirmed by its connection with different female figures. There are, however, certain prefixes and suffixes which may serve to give it a specific application; for example, in LXVII, 14, from Dres. 16c, the prefix, according to my interpretation, contains the *z* sound as its chief phonetic element. It is possible that in this case a particular person may be referred to by the prefix, the woman symbol being here simply a determinative. Dr Brinton, in his explanation of the month name *Zip*, remarks: "This was *Zuhuy Zip*, the virgin *Zip*, her name being properly *Itzip*, 'to skin, to dress slain animals.'" I prefer, however, to interpret the symbol by "maiden," or "young woman," the prefix signifying *zuhuy*. Nevertheless, the suffix in some instances, as LXVII, 15, from Dres. 18b, may indicate that a sacred or mythological personage is referred to, as it is added as a suffix in some cases to deity symbols; however, as it is often found in other relations, where it can have no such signification. I am not inclined to give it this interpretation, as the evident female deities are denoted by quite different glyphs.

The evidence that the Caban symbol is in some sense phonetic appears to me to be too strong to be rejected. In the first place, one of its chief elements is the corkscrew figure, which, as shown under the preceding day, appears to have *b* as its consonant element, this sound

being a prominent element of both *cib* and *caban*. It also has been
shown that it is not out of place in the woman glyph, under the supposition that this is also phonetic, as *ckup* or *ckupal* is the Maya name for
woman, and the change from b to p is not uncommon. It is found in several places as that one of which plants are growing, as LXVII, 16, from
Tro. 33b, which appears to represent some leguminous plant supported
by a stake driven into the ground. It is that on which persons are
sitting Indian fashion, and on which others are lying; again, it is that
out of which a serpent is arising. As "earth," "ground," will furnish
an entirely satisfactory explanation in all these cases, there is no apparent reason why it should not be accepted. As *cab* has "earth" as one
of its leading significations, we not only find therein a connection with
the day name, but also an indication of phoneticism.

In Cort. 30a is the figure shown at LXVII, 17. The animal represented,
notwithstanding the quadruped head, is conceded to be intended for
the serpent. The shading around the vessel, a blotch of which is on
the serpent's nose, I take for the clay or paste out of which the vessel
is being formed, or to be formed. In the division immediately below is
a representation of what appears to be some step in the manufacture of
vessels. May this not be correctly interpreted by *kancab*, "in terra roja
o amarilla," or "red clay!" Henderson gives *cancou* as an equivalent
term of *kankan*. As I have not seen a copy of the colored edition of
this codex, I can not say whether this interpretation is borne out by
the color of the shading. If this interpretation be correct, the serpent
figure must be used symbolically or as a true rebus.

In Tro. 9*c an individual is represented lifting what is supposed to
be honey or honeycomb out of a box-shaped object on which is the
caban symbol. This symbol is presumed to indicate the contents—
"honey." If this supposition be correct, then, as *cab* is the Maya name
for "honey," we have in this coincidence in *caual* and glyph another
indication of phoneticism. Support is given to this interpretation by
the fact that this is found in what is known as the "bee section," and
that on the upper division of the same plate the same figure, with the
codex symbol upon it, is seen in the hands of an individual who holds
it to a bee.

As the character when used otherwise than a day symbol is frequently,
perhaps most generally, drawn with a suffix, as shown in LXVII, 18, I suggest that it is possible it is a conventional method of representing earth
or soil. By reference to the Borgian Codex, plate 11, also 10a and 61b,
it will be seen that where earth is introduced into the picture it is indicated by heavy and wavy lines, as shown in LXVII, 19. This bears a
very strong resemblance to the suffix of LXVII, 18. The corkscrew or root
figure is added as appropriate, as an element, in forming an earth figure.
Such, I am inclined to believe, is the origin of the symbol which, when
used to indicate anything else than earth, is used phonetically or
ikonomatically. The figure shown in LXVII, 20, from Dres. 36c, which
Seler calls a serpent, is merely the representation of a clay image and

the seat or oratorio in which it is placed. It is probably from something of comparatively small size, burnt in one piece. The mark of the earth symbol, to distinguish the substance of which it is made, is certainly appropriate. In Tro. 6b we see another on which is quite a different symbol, indicating, as will hereafter be shown, that the material is wood.

The compound character in LXVII, 21, is found in Tro. 9*b and 10*c. It occurs in the latter twice, the parts, however, reversed in the parallel groups, while in that of 9*b one is above the other. These variants do not necessarily indicate a difference in the signification, as can readily be ascertained by comparing characters in the numerous parallel groups. Omitting the prefix, this may be rendered suk-cub, "to eat honey without chewing (that is, by sucking); to break into a hive and steal the honey." By reference to the plates on which the symbols are found the appropriateness of this rendering will be apparent, if I rightly interpret the figures below the text. There we see the twisted red symbols denoting the fire kindled beneath the hives, or beehouses, by which to drive out or destroy the busy little workers. In one of the fires we observe bone symbols, probably denoting a method of giving to the smoke an unpleasant odor, as rags were formerly used in some sections of our country for the same purpose.

The characters shown in LXVII, 22 and 23, are from the upper part of Cort. 22, which is supposed to be the right half of the so-called "title page" of the Tro. Codex. These are interpreted by Seler, and probably correctly, as indicating "above" and "below" (LXVII, 22, the former, and LXVII, 23, the latter). By following the line in which these characters are found, through the two pages, beginning at the left of the plate of the Tro. Codex, the result appears to be as follows, giving the signification of the characters so far as known: First, the four cardinal points in one direction, then two characters apparently corresponding with the two we have figured, one of which is partly obliterated; next the cardinal points in an opposite direction, after which follow the two characters shown in LXVII, 22 and 23. As the right half of the first (22) is the cab or caban symbol, it is presumable that it has here substantially the same phonetic value. It is probable, therefore, that the whole compound character may be rendered yokcabil (or okcabil), "above the earth," or as Henderson, who gives two words of this form, interprets the first, "over, above the earth, above." The second (LXVII, 23) has also as its chief part the cab symbol, and the upper right-hand portion appears to have x'u as its chief phonetic elements. It is possible that cabaix "a stair," "downward," given by Henderson, furnishes the phonetic equivalent of the compound character. These six directions, according to Dr J. W. Fewkes,[1] were noted by the Tusayan Indians in some of their religious ceremonies. Mr Cushing says the same thing is true in regard to some of the Zuñi ceremonies.

[1] Jour. Am. Eth. and Arch., II, p. 30.

Plate LXVII, 24, is a compound character from Dres. 39b, below which the long-nose deity holds in his hand a peculiar article (LXVII, 25), "as if," says Seler, "pouring out of a bottle." That the prefix has the interior cross-hatched when complete appears from a number of other places, as, for example, in the upper division of the same plate. This, as heretofore stated, gives the *x* or *sh* sound. It is possible, therefore, that the symbol, omitting the right portion, should be interpreted *xechoob*, "a little de par en par," or *xechcab*, "to open little by little, to develop, discover it" (Henderson). As the right portion has a character resembling the *Muluc* symbol as its chief element, and below it the *u* glyph, we may translate it *muyal*, "cloud." This would give as the meaning of the entire symbol "open the cloud"—that is, "to pour out the rain." As this is connected with a rain series, and we see a similar glyph (though with different prefix) on plate 38b, where the same deity is in the midst of a rain storm and holding in his hand a similar object, the rendering appears to be, at least, appropriate. It is to be further observed that this combined *Cabau* and *Muluc* symbol is found frequently in connection with rain storms and cloud symbols.

According to the interpretation given LXVII, 22 and 24, the compound symbol shown at 26, from Dres. 35b and 34b, should be rendered *Yokenbil muyal*, "the cloud above." As we see in both places, in the picture under the text, the looped serpent inclosing water, which Dr Seler considers the "water sack" or cloud, this interpretation is appropriate. As further confirmation of the interpretation given LXVII, 22, attention is called to the picture in Tro. 32*c over which the same symbol is found. Here the allusion is doubtless to the basket-like covering over, or "above," the black deity lying on a mat.

THE EIGHTEENTH DAY

Maya, *eiznab* or *eznab*; Tzental, *chinax*; Quiche-Cakchiquel, *tihax*; Zapotec, *gopaa*; Nahuatl, *tecpatl*.

The form of the symbol of this day varies but little in the codices, as shown by plate LXVII, 28–31. It is seldom found in this form in combination. If its equivalent is given in these, it is of the form shown in 33. It is, however, occasionally seen on articles of stone, as the spearpoint (32) and stone hatchet (34) and sacrificial knife. It also appears in the symbol for the stone mortar (36) from Tro. 19c. Before discussing its signification and probable origin we will give the significations which have been suggested of the different names of the day.

The signification of the Nahuatl name—*tecpatl*—is "flint." Dr Brinton says, "especially the flint-stone knife used in sacrificing, to cut the victim." Dr Seler finds agreement in the Tzental name from a statement, by Nuñez de la Vega, that the symbol *chinax*, or rather the tutelary god of the same, was a great warrior, who was always represented in the calendars with a banner in his hand, and that he was slain and burned by the nagual of another heathen symbol. Dr Brinton states

COPIES OF GLYPHS FROM THE CODICES

that the name "is an old or sacred form of the naual *zab-nex*, 'knife.'" The literal meaning of the Cakchiquel *tihax* is, according to Ximenes, "it bites, scraping" (muerde rasgando). Dr Seler, however, affirms that Ximenes (with what authority he knows not) gives "obsidian" as the meaning. He thinks the word is related to the root *tenk*, "cold"— *tik-ik*, "to be cold"—with which may be compared the words *tic*, "to stick in, prick;" *tiz*, "to stitch," and *tzalic*, "pointed."

In regard to the Zapotec name, *gopaa*, *gopaa*, or *opaa*, the authors named differ quite widely, Dr Seler deriving it from *rogopa*, "cold," and Dr Brinton suggesting that it is more likely "a variant of *guipa*, a sharp point or edge, whence the word for stone knife, *guexa-guipa*, from *guia*, stone."

The Maya name, however, does not appear to be readily brought into harmony with the others. Dr Seler simply remarks that it may be related to the root *e*, "firm, rigid, hard." Pio Perez offers no explanation. Dr Brinton suggests that it is a figurative expression for the sacrificial knife, from *nab*, something anointed, or blood, and *edz*, to adjust, to point, to sharpen.

There can be no question that the articles in the codices on which the trembling cross is found consists, in most instances, if not all, of stone. Hence it is a reasonable conclusion that the primary signification of the symbol is stone. The Zotzil name for "flint" (pedernal) is *chitox*.

I am inclined to believe that the symbol is derived from a conventional form used for indicating stone or flint, probably from the cracks or fissures in it.

I am not prepared yet to discuss the somewhat similar figures which assume the form of the St Anthony cross. Various interpretations, as symbol for "union," "night sun," etc, have been given. However, as this form is never used as a day symbol, it has no direct relation to the present discussion.

THE NINETEENTH DAY

Maya, *cauac*; Tzental, *aakogh*; Quiche-Cakchiquel, *caok*, *took*; Zapotec, *ape*, *appe*, *aape*; Kakchatl, *quiahuitl*.

The various forms of the symbol of this day are shown in plate LXVII, 37–48—that by Landa at 37; those of the Troano and Cortesian codices at 38–43, and those from the Dresden Codex at 45–47. The irregular form given at 44 is from Tro. 28d, and that at 48 from the Peresianus.

This symbol is found quite frequently in combination with other characters, in some of which its phonetic value can be ascertained with reasonable certainty. For example, it forms the lower half of the symbol for the month *Yax*, as seen at LXIV, 12; also in the symbol for the month *Zac* (LXVI, 48). In both these instances its chief phonetic element appears to be the guttural sound *k*, or *kz*. The essential elements are also found frequently on objects which are undoubtedly of wood and where no reasonable explanation can be given except that it signifies "wood" in these places. For example, it is found on what appear to

be boards carried in the hands of individuals, on Tro. 32*b (LXVII, 49);
and it also is seen on what appear to be wooden boxes or gums from
which the honeycomb is being removed, as Tro. 5*c and 0*a. Dr Seler,
who gives quite a different interpretation of the character from that
presented here, admits that these are boards. It is also found on trees,
as Tro. 15*a (shown in LXVIII, 1) and 17*a, and Dres. 26c, 27c, and 28c.
It is marked on the walls of houses or canopied seats, as Tro. 6b, 20*c,
and 18*b. Under the last mentioned we observe the cab symbol, showing that it is a building placed on the ground and not on a stone foundation. It also appears on the ends of beams, as at Tro. 9a and 22*a.
True, Dr Seler contends that these are stones instead of weight poles,
but I think all trappers will decide against him. Again, it appears on
seats (Tro. 13a and 14*a) and also marked on heads, one of which is
shown in LXVIII, 2. That the symbol is not intended to indicate the different articles on which it is found is evident; hence it must be given to
denote the substance of which these things are formed, which I main-
tain can only be wood. That the trees and boards must be wood is
admitted; that the walls of many of the houses and of some of the
other buildings of Yucatan were of wood must be admitted; that seats
were often of wood is well known. The heads with this mark are in all
probability representations of wooden masks. Masks are represented
in the hands of individuals at several places in the codices, as Dres.
42(1)a and in Peresianus. I therefore conclude that in all these cases
the symbol is to be interpreted by *che, cheil*, "wood, tree, timber, stick."

In order to show the difference between the explanation given here
and that by Dr Seler, I copy the latter:

We find, for instance, on the one hand the undoubted application which is connected with the idea of stone or rain. Thus, in the hieroglyph, figure 80, the accompanying hieroglyph of figure 46, i. e., the bird Moan. So also the one in figure 28
(p. 107) the accompanying hieroglyph of the name Kinchahau, which, besides canac,
contains further the element of fire and that of the hatchet, which may remind us of
the ray (or flash) darting from the cloud. The hieroglyph canac is, however, used
far more commonly in the sense of "stone" or "heaviness." This is most clearly
shown in the case of the animal figures pictured in Cod. Tro. 9a and 22*a, where the
stone laid upon and weighing down the horizontal beam is represented by the element
canac. But this explanation must be accepted also, because we find the pyramidal
foundation of the temple covered with the element canac. And where, in Cod. Tro.
15*a, in the Chac who is felling a tree is opposed the death god, also felling a tree,
covered by the element canac, it is clear that here there is substituted with the death
god a rigid stone in place of what with the Chac is a sprouting tree. The numerous
cases in which the hieroglyph canac serves as a seat or footstool of the gods are sometimes easily interpreted as signifying clouds, but in the majority of cases it undoubtedly represents "stone," homologous to the hieroglyph caban and the element tun,
"stone," itself (figure 85), both of which are found equally often denoting the seat
and footstool of the gods. It is equally evident that in the hieroglyph figure 84, in
which there is indicated the bearing of a burden on the back, the element canac is
to be understood simply as the expression of the weight, the burden. In the peculiar
cases where we see the gods holding a board provided with the elements of the character canac, or where a board is placed before the gods, furnished with a plaited handle
whose side bears the element canac, the latter seems to relate to a sounding board,
for the accompanying hieroglyphs seem to signify music. Finally, there can be

found a direct homology between the element canac and the element tun. This is seen in the hieroglyph of the hunting god of figure 83, whose distinguishing mark is usually an eye or the element tun (i. e., a precious stone), which he bears in the front of the headdress. The hieroglyph of this god is written sometimes as in figure 81, sometimes as figure 83. And that the element here, which in figure 83 replaces the element canac, is to be understood in fact as tun or "stone, precious stone," is evident, on the one hand from the application of the precious stone in the headdress (tun, "piedra, piedra preciosa"), and, on the other hand, from its use as the base of the pole on which Mam, the Payayab demon, is set up during the xma kaba kin (Cod. Dres. 25c). Now, it is true that a connection of ideas can be established with considerable certainty between clouds, rain, and stone, for in that region every rain was a thunderstorm. But at the same time it will be found comprehensible that a barrier of doubt was removed when I discovered in the course of my Zapotec studies that in Zapotec the same word was used for "rain" and "stone," namely, *quia, quir.*

According to the explanation I have given above, the chief phonetic element of the character is the guttural sound *k, kx* (or *r*), and *ch*. As additional evidence tending to confirm this conclusion, the following examples are given:

Symbols 61, LXV, from Tro. 23*a, and 62, from Dres. 1 (42), have already been explained, the first as signifying *kutz* or *cutz,* "the turkey," and the second *tzac,* the name of a certain fish found in the senotes. In the first (61) the first or left-hand character is our *Canac* symbol and has the *k* sound, and the same symbol forms the right portion in the second (62) and also has the *k* sound. In LXVI, 47, from Dres. 18c, the *Canac* symbol forms the first or upper portion. The whole compound symbol, as above shown, may be consistently interpreted *cuckpach,* "a porter or carrier;" literally, "one who bears on the back." Again we see the *k* sound given the character is consistent. The symbol for the month *Cch,* as found in the Dresden Codex, is shown at LXVI, 44. In this the last or lower portion is also the *Canac* character, and, according to the value assigned it, should have a harder sound than the simple aspirate. That such is the case is rendered probable by the fact that Henderson gives *erh* and *kex* both as names of the month and as Maya words for "deer." In the Zotzil *chigh* is the name for "deer." It is therefore apparent that the symbol has here the guttural sound.

The glyphs in LXVII, 50 and 51 (Cort. 21), probably signify "night" and "evening"; the first (50), *akab,* "night," and the second (51), *kuakin,* one signification of which, according to Henderson, is "evening." The wing-like appendage is probably a time determinative. These last interpretations are of course given with some doubt. However, this may be said in their favor, that wing-like appendages are usually attached to time symbols, and that the figures below the text represent persons, each of whom carries what appears to be a wheel, possibly like those used in keeping time, and the main character of the preceding symbol in both cases is the *Manik* glyph, having *ch* as its chief phonetic element and *chackinib,* signifying "hours, wheel." Precisely the same symbol as LXVII, 51, preceded by the *Manik* glyph, and a wheel in the hand of the person figured below the text, is seen in Troano 35d.

The character shown in LXVII, 52, from Tro. 35c, may possibly be correctly rendered by *bakah* (*baakal*), "to roll round about, to go round about," alluding to the flight of the vulture figured below the text. This supposition appears to be strengthened by the probable interpretation of the symbol immediately below it (LXVII, 53), *malaalahak*, "without repeated bufetings." The character given in LXVII, 3, from Tro. 31a, may be interpreted *pak*, "to sow seed, to plant," and that shown in LXVIII, 4, from the second division of the same plate, indicates the same word, as the transposition of the parts of a symbol does not always indicate a change of signification. Possibly, however, its equivalent may be *capak*, "to reseed or sow seed the second time," or *kapak*, "to place in a trench or hole." As the persons figured below the text appear to be planting seed by dibbling them in with a stick, this would seem to be an appropriate rendering. Dr Seler appears to have entirely misunderstood these figures, as he thinks they represent the deities pouring out water. I have in a previous part of this paper given some reasons for believing that these plates refer to the planting and cultivation of corn.

These examples will suffice at this point.

It is difficult to decide as to the origin of the glyph. However, I am inclined to believe it has grown out of a conventional symbol for wood, possibly drawn from the little knots and marks seen on the inside surface of split wood. This may be wide of the true explanation, but all the indications I can find point in this direction. As "wood" (*leño*) in Zotzil (I do not know what it is in Tzental) is *ci*—equal to *ki* or *gi*— we obtain the guttural sound which appears to be the chief element of the symbol. In its use it appears to shade off from the hard to the soft sound.

The Zapotec name *ape*, which, according to Dr Brinton, may properly be translated by "lightning," or "the lightning flash," is much like the name for "fire" which prevails throughout Oceanica. Commencing with the Malay *api*, we trace it through the Oceanic islands in such forms as *api*, *iap*, *yap*, *uap*, *yaf*; to New Zealand *kapura*; Tonga and Samoan *afi*, and Hawaiian *ahi*.

In the Zapotec words *lsari-api-nixa* and *ri-api-lahu*, translated "relampago, relampaguear," we find precisely the original form of the Oceanic word for "fire."

THE TWENTIETH DAY

Maya, ahau; Tzental, aghual; Quiche-Cakchiquel, hunahpu; Zapotec, lao or loo; Nahuatl, xochitl.

The symbol for this day, except where evidently imperfectly drawn, is subject to but few and slight changes, that given by Landa corresponding to the form found in the codices.

The usual and correct form is shown in LXVIII, 5-7; slight variations are seen in LXVIII, 8 and 9. Dr Seler figures several other varieties, but

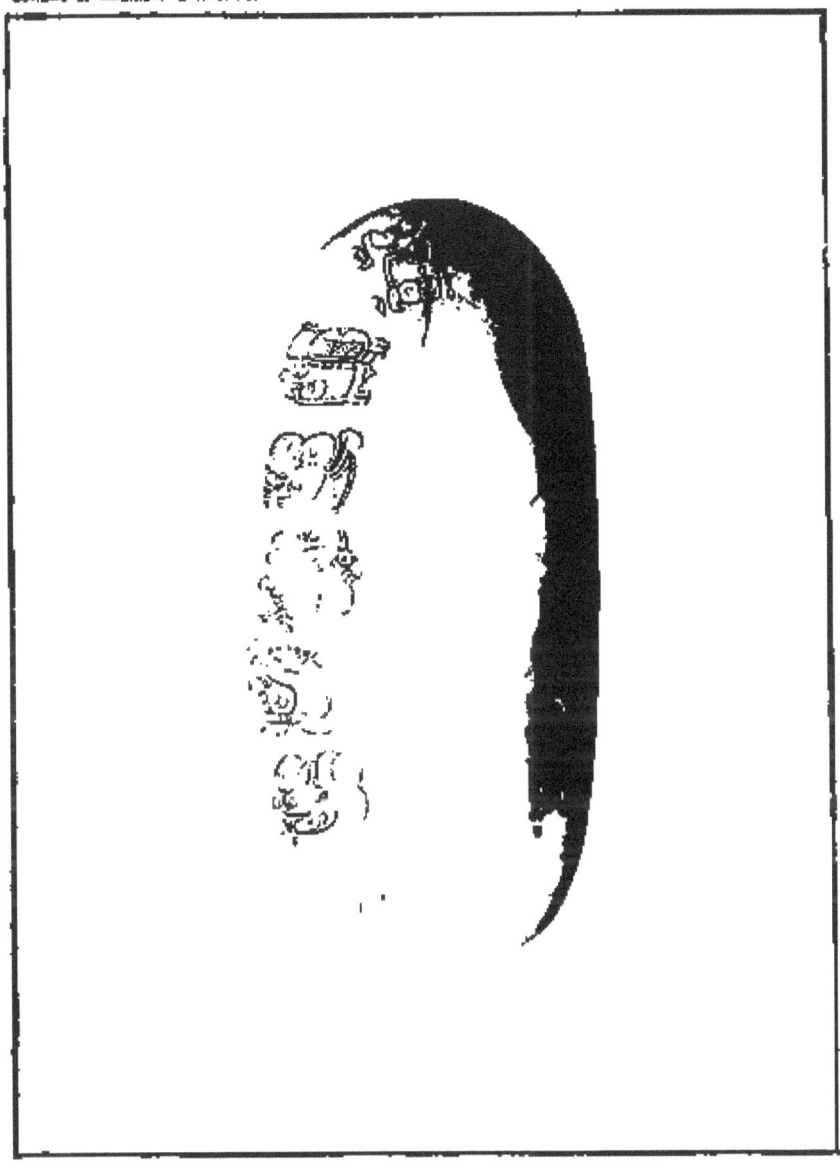

SHELL BEARING MAYA GLYPHS

as these are from plates of the Dresden Codex, where the symbol is in columns, where they are evidently hastily made, without any attempt to have more than one or two in a column complete, they are not given here. The character represented in LXVIII, 10, is from the Tikal inscription, and that in LXVIII, 11, from the Palenque Tablet.

The Maya and Tzental names signify "king, lord, sovereign." The derivation of the word has been explained in various ways. Brasseur explains it by "the lord of the collar," *ah-au*, as does Dr Brinton; Stoll gives "lord of the cultivated lands," from the Ixil, *araau*, "to sow." Dr Seler, however, is disposed to derive the name from the masculine prefix *ah* and *ninic* or *rinak*, "man." His method of reaching this conclusion is as follows:

For the Tzental word *aghaal*, standing parallel with the Maya *ahau*, which doubtless corresponds to the abstract form *ahaual* of the word *ahau*, is to be referred rather to a primitive form *au*, *a'hu*, *ahu*, than to *ahua*. In the Tzental Pater Noster which Pimentel gives, we find the phrase "to come Thy kingdom (Thy dominion)" expressed by the words *ocu talac le agualuic*. The primitive meaning of *ahau* is certainly "man," "lord," and the two roots of similar significance, *ah* and *au* (see *alalc*, *rinak*, "man") seem to concur in this word.

He explains the Quiche-Cakchiquel *hunahpu* by *hun*, "one," and *ahpu* "lord of the blowpipe," or "blowpipe shooter." Dr Brinton translates it the "One Master of Power." He brings the Mexican name into harmony by rendering it "the flower of the day"—that is, the sun; and the Zapotec by rendering it "eye," meaning "the eye of the day"—i. e., the sun.

When we attempt to bring the symbol of the day into harmony with the Maya name, we encounter a difficulty which can be overcome only by following a different line from that suggested by Dr Brinton or Dr Seler. That the character shown in LXVIII, 12, is the symbol for the cardinal point "east," which in Maya is *likin*, is now generally admitted, and that the lower portion is the symbol for *kin*, "day" or "sun," is also admitted. We are therefore justified in concluding that the upper portion, which is the *Ahau* symbol, stands for *li*, and that *l* is its consonant element. If Landa's second *l* (shown in LXVIII, 43) is turned part way round, it will be seen that it is a rough attempt to draw the *Ahau* symbol. If a careful study is made of his *l*s as given in his list, and his example of spelling *le*, and of the similar characters in the codices, it will be seen that both his *l* characters are derived from the same original. For example, the character shown in LXV, 60, from Tro. 22*a is precisely the combination which this author translates *le*, "a snare," or "to snare." By referring to the plate it will be seen that it is followed by the character (LXV, 61) which we have interpreted *kutz*, "turkey," and that in the picture below the text there is a lassoed turkey. It is apparent, therefore, that both these forms are used sometimes for words of which *l* is the chief phonetic element, and that the parallelogram and two interior dots are the essential elements. The day symbol is of less frequency in combination than the other form, but it sometimes occurs. It must, however, be distinguished from the closely allied *p* symbol heretofore alluded to.

From what has been shown in regard to the symbol, it would seem, if considered phonetic, that the original day name it was intended to represent contained *l* as its chief consonant element. If ikonomatic, the name of the thing indicated had *l* as its chief element.

I think there can be little doubt that the symbol, as has been suggested by others, was taken from the full face, the central double line representing the nose, the two open dots the eyes, and the circle below the mouth. Now, according to Fuller's Zapotec Vocabulary, the name for face is *lu*, which is the Zapotec name of the day. As has been stated, Dr Brinton thinks the Nahuatl and Zapotec names refer to the sun, and he is inclined also to believe that the "ruler" or "sovereign" referred to by the names of the Maya dialects is the sun.

I think we may rest assured that the symbol of this day was derived from the full face, and that the word (for face) it was intended to indicate had *l* as its chief phonetic element—possibly from *lec*, "brow, front, forehead." If derived from the face, its use as a day symbol, and in numerous combinations, proves beyond question that it is phonetic in the true or in the rebus sense.

APPENDIX

1. Tane was the parent of the tui, of birds in general, and trees.
2. Ru, the father of lakes and rivers.
3. Rupe, of the pigeon.
4. Tangaroa, of fish.
5. Irawaru, of dogs.
6. Nga rangi-hora, of stones.
7. Mauika, of fire.
8. Maui, of the land.
9. Muwakenga, of the Totara; also called Takau moana.
10. Parari, of the Tui (bird).
11. Papa, of the Kiwi [Apteryx Australis].
12. Owa. of the dog; he was also the father of Irawaru.
13. Pakihi, of the Kaka.
14. Punga Matao, of the shark (mationi), lizard, and tanuci (the mapperch-fish).
15. Tuto meron, of the Kahikatoa [a plant so named].
16. Hine-maki, of the rat.
17. Turanhore, of the Kahikatea [a certain tree] and Rimu [a species of pine].
18. Hara-ara-one, of the Weka [a large bird].
19. Rongo, of the Kumara (sweet potato); also called Rongomatane.
20. Tiki, of man.
21. Tara-aga-mein, of evil.
22. Tahu, of all good.
23. Tawhri-matea, of the winds.
24. Motolkwewra, of lizards.
25. (Hanei-rangi, of the palm tree (nikau) and flax (harakeke).
26. Haumia, of the fern root.
27. Tomairangi, of dew.
28. Haupapa, of ice.
29. Hauhunga. of cold.
30. Tawpo hau, father of storm and tempests.

It must be understood that these are not the names of the days, but of the deities which preside over them, and of the things which they created or of which they had special care.

TUSAYAN SNAKE CEREMONIES

BY

JESSE WALTER FEWKES

CONTENTS

	Page
Introductory note	273
The Cipaulovi snake ceremony	277
General remarks	277
The Antelope altar	278
The ceremonies on the day called totokya	279
The Antelope dance	281
The Snake race	282
The Snake dance	284
The Cuñopavi snake ceremony	287
General remarks	287
The Antelope altar	287
The Snake dance	288
The Oraïbi snake ceremony	290
General remarks	290
The Antelope altar	290
The Antelope dance	292
The Snake race	293
The Snake dance	293
Differences in accessories	295
General remarks	295
Pahos	295
The kisi	297
Snake whips	297
Snake kilts	297
Theoretic deductions	298
Resemblances to the Keresan Snake dance	301
Bibliography	312

ILLUSTRATIONS

	Page
PLATE LXX. The Snake dance at Cipaulovi. a, The pahoki or shrine in the plaza. b, The kisi	278
LXXI. Altar of the Antelope priests at Cipaulovi	281
LXXII. Altar of the Antelope priests at Cuñopavi	280
LXXIII. Altar of the Antelope priests at Oraibi	281
LXXIV. The Antelope dance at Oraibi. a, Entrance and circuit of the Antelope priests. b, Entrance of the Snake priests	292
LXXV. The Antelope dance at Oraibi. a, Platoons of Antelope and Snake priests at the opening of the dance. b, Snake priests shaking their whips	293
LXXVI. The Antelope dance at Oraibi. a, Line of Antelope priests. b, The asperger carrying the wad of cornstalks and bean vines	292
LXXVII. The Snake dance at Oraibi. a, Entrance of the Antelope priests. b, Circuit of the Antelope priests before the kisi	294
LXXVIII. The Snake dance at Oraibi. a, Antelope priests awaiting the Snake priests at the kisi. b, Preliminary circuit of the Snake priests in the Antelope dance	294
LXXIX. The Snake dance at Oraibi. a, The dance before the reptiles are taken from the kisi. b, The snake carrier and the hugger	294
LXXX. Snake priests with reptiles. a, The Oraibi performance. b, The Cipaulovi performance	296
LXXXI. Diagram showing positions of kivas, kisis, shrines, and participants in the snake ceremonials. a, Walpi. b, Cipaulovi. c, Cuñopavi. d, Oraibi	289

TUSAYAN SNAKE CEREMONIES

By Jesse Walter Fewkes

INTRODUCTORY NOTE

When I began my studies of the Snake dance at Walpi, in 1891, it was said by all the white men whom I consulted that this weird ceremony was confined to the pueblos of Walpi and Micoñinovi, and there was no mention in the literature dealing with the subject of its existence in other villages of Tusayan. During the course of my researches,[1] however, it was discovered that the same or a closely related ceremony takes place in even years at Oraibi and Cuñopavi, and considerable material was collected regarding the exhibition in the latter village in 1892. Shortly after the publication of my memoir[2] on the Snake ceremonials of Walpi, attention was called to the existence of a similar rite in Cipaulovi, so that we are now cognizant of its celebration in five Tusayan villages—Walpi, Micoñinovi, Cuñopavi, Cipaulovi, and Oraibi. As the remaining two pueblos, Sitcomovi and Hano, are now known not to have a Snake dance, we have exact information concerning the Tusayan villages where this ceremony is observed.

The ever-increasing interest in the Snake dance of the Hopi dates from the description by the late Captain J. G. Bourke in 1884. Since the publication of Bourke's valuable book, many articles of more or less scientific value have appeared, so that this rite has now come to be one of the best known of all aboriginal American ceremonials. Most of these accounts, however, deal with the Walpi presentation, and there is a wide field of research still uncultivated in the other pueblos.

The Snake dance at Micoñinovi was first described by Mr Cosmos Mindeleff,[3] and although it has been witnessed by many persons since his article appeared, the ceremony still remains one of the most obscure of all these presentations.

The first notice of the Snake dance at Oraibi we owe to Mr J. H. Politzer, of Phœnix, Arizona, who published numerous newspaper

---

[1] These studies were made in 1896, while the author was connected with the Bureau of American Ethnology.

[2] Journal of American Ethnology and Archæology, Vol. iv.

[3] Science, Vol. vii, June 4, 1886.

accounts of the 1891 presentation, which may be consulted in files of that date. In 1892 Mr R. H. Baxter observed parts of the Oipaulovi or Onllopovi dances and published a short notice of them in the *American Antiquarian*. It can hardly be said, however, that the accounts by Politzer and Baxter advanced our knowledge of the Snake dance to any considerable degree, as the secret ceremonials were wholly neglected and the public events superficially, often inaccurately, described. They have a value, however, in verifying the statements which had already been made after personal observation of the dances in these three pueblos. Mr Politzer's photographs showed an unexpected fact, that the numbers of participants in the Ornibi dance were small, a feature on which I have elsewhere commented.

From reasons which need not be enumerated, the majority of the descriptions of the Tusayan Snake dance have been limited to the exhibition at Walpi, and our knowledge of this variant far exceeds that of the other pueblos. It is, therefore, but natural that the Walpi dance should be regarded as the most complicated, and while extended research tends to support such a conclusion, it does not necessarily demonstrate that the ceremony at Walpi is the most primitive, but rather tends to show the reverse. To obtain what light we can on this point, as a preliminary to generalizations in regard to the nature and meaning of the Tusayan Snake dance, it is desirable to investigate the details of the presentation in the villages where our knowledge is more fragmentary. The present article is, therefore, offered as a contribution to a study of the Snake dances of Ornibi, Oipaulovi, and Onllopavi, with generalizations which, it is believed, are warranted by new data obtained from these observations.

The duration of the Snake dance ceremonial at Walpi, where it is celebrated in the most elaborated form, may be stated as twenty days, of which only nine days are marked by active ceremonials, secret or open. Sixteen days before the Snake dance occurs it is formally announced, and on the preceding night the chiefs gather, engage in ceremonial smoking, and commission the town crier to call out the date on the following sunrise.[1] The next seven days are not days of ceremony, although the Antelope chief is engaged in preparations. The eighth day (on which he and others enter the kiva, or "*pahit*," as it is called) is the *yũñya*, or assembly, and for nine days the secret ceremonials continue, closing at sunset of the ninth day by a dance in the plaza, when snakes are carried in the mouths of the participants. The following four days are included in my enumeration, as they are days of purification, but are conspicuous to public eyes only as the frolics, called *niñties*, which I have described elsewhere. If these different components are rightly embraced by me in the Snake ceremony, we have, in the twenty days' proceedings, five groups of four days each;

---

or, beginning with the last, four days of frolic, four days from the erection of the Snake altar to the Snake dance, four days from the erection of the Antelope altar to the making of the Snake altar, and eight inactive days, which I am unable to separate by any distinct events.

The nine days of ceremony, beginning with yáñya and ending with the dance, have a nomenclature suggestive of a division into two groups of four each. The day after the assembly is called the "first day" (cüctala). Then follow the "second day" (lüctala), the "third day" (paictala), and the "fourth day" (nalactala). The second series then begins with a second cüctala, or "first day," closing with the public dance.[1] On this basis it will be seen that the number four, so constant in pueblo ritual, is prominent in the number of days in the Snake ceremonial. I will call attention also to the fact that the nine days of ceremonies plus the four days of frolic make the mystic number thirteen. It may likewise be borne in mind that the period of twenty days, the theoretical length of the most elaborate Tusayan ceremony, was also characteristic of other more cultured peoples in Mexico, and that thirteen ceremonials, each twenty days long, make a year of 260 days, a ceremonial epoch of the Maya and related peoples.

The comparative studies which are here considered deal with portions only of the rites of the nine days. This has been necessary on account of the poverty of data at my control. There seems abundant evidence that in the three pueblos considered there is no such complexity of secret rites as at Walpi, and consequently there are abbreviations. Thus the Antelope altar at Oraibi is not erected on yáñya, as at Walpi, while at Cipaulovi it is made on the second cüctala, or only four days before the dance. When we know all the details of the Snake ceremonials in each of the five Tusayan pueblos, we shall be able to draw our comparisons much more closely than at present. This article, therefore, is preliminary, a temporary summary, or a step, it is hoped, toward a more exact knowledge of the Snake dances in all the pueblos of Tusayan.

The dates of the nine days on which ceremonials belonging to the Snake dances were observed in 1896, at the three villages, are as follows (the presence of the author is indicated by an asterisk):

	Oraibi	Cipaulovi	Cuñopavi
Yañya	August 11	August 15*	August 16
Cüctala	August 12	August 16	August 17
Lüctala	August 13	August 17	August 18
Paictala	August 14	August 18	August 19
Naloctala	August 15	August 19	August 20
Cüctala	August 16	August 20	August 21
Komoktotokya	August 17*	August 21*	August 22
Totokya	August 18*	August 22*	August 23
Tihüne	August 19*	August 23*	August 24*

[1] Journ. Amer. Eth. and Archæol., Vol. IV, pp. 13, 14, note.

The secret rites at Cipaulovi took place in the two kivas, the one at the right as one enters the pueblo from Micoñinovi being occupied by the Antelope priests, that on the western side being used by the Snake priests. The Antelope kiva was the same as that occupied by the Katcina chief in the *Niñdakatcina*, as I have elsewhere described.[1] The two kivas used at Cuñopavi are at the entrance of the pueblo, that to the left being occupied by the Antelope priests, the one to the right by the Snake priests. The two Oraibi kivas occupied in the Snake dance were on the western side, the one to the right as one emerges from the village being used by the Antelopes, that on the left by the Snake priests.

[1] Journ. Amer. Eth. and Archæol., Vol. ii, No. 1, pp. 49-162.

THE CIPAULOVI SNAKE CEREMONY

GENERAL REMARKS

It has elsewhere been shown that the Snake dance is announced sixteen days before its celebration, after a formal smoke by the chiefs on the preceding night. The nine days of active ceremonials are composed of seven days of secret observances and two of public exhibitions in which dances in the plaza occur. One of these takes place on the eighth day, and has been called the Antelope;[1] the other, on the ninth, is known as the Snake dance proper. The nomenclature of these nine days at Walpi has likewise been given, and the same holds in regard to the days of Snake ceremonials at Cipaulovi, Cuñopavi, and Oraibi. On August 10, the *chülala*, or first day at Cipaulovi, I visited both Antelope and Snake kivas of this pueblo, but found no altar there. This was exceptional, as compared with Walpi, at the very outset, for in this pueblo the altar is made on the assembly day (*yuñya*). The Antelope chief was present in the kiva, and a bundle of sticks was noticed at the rear end of the room, leaning against the wall. These sticks were the crooks which were later set about the altar in a way which will be described. The chief said the altar would not be made for four days—a statement which I afterward verified—and he added that the Snake dance would occur in eight days. While I was talking with the Antelope chief, the Snake chief came in, and smoked in a formal way; and at the close of the smoke the Antelope chief gave him three strings with red stained feathers tied at their ends (known as *nakwakwocis*), and a small white feather. When the Snake chief received them, he sprinkled a little sacred meal on the bundle of sticks and returned to his own kiva.

So far as I could judge, this ceremony corresponded to the delivery of the prayer-sticks (*pahos*) to Kopeli, the Snake chief, when he went on the snake hunt which I have elsewhere described at length,[2] for the Snake priests immediately set forth on a snake hunt northward from the pueblo. For the next four days this simple ceremony of delivery of the feathered strings to the Snake chief was repeated, and the Snake priests hunted reptiles in the remaining world-quarters, west, south, and east, in the proscribed circuit.

---

[1] The "Oraibi Flute Altar" (see the Bibliography at the date of the article). Strictly speaking, this dance should be called the Corn dance; but as the corn-growing element of the Snake ceremonial is limited to the Antelope priesthood, I retain the name Antelope dance for the public exhibition on the eighth day.

[2] Journ. Amer. Eth. and Archæol., Vol. IV, pp. 40, 41.

There was a small kotci, made of two sticks tied together, set in the straw matting of each kiva, as at Walpi, and the snake whips of the Snake kiva were arranged upright in a row leaning against the rear wall. This row of snake whips was the only feature comparable with an altar that was constructed in the Snake chamber of Cipaulovi.

As I was obliged to spend the following days at Micoñinovi, studying the Flute observance, no further visits were made to the Cipaulovi kivas until August 21, or the day called Lowoktotolya, when I saw the Antelope altar for the first time, it having been made apparently either that morning or the day before.[1] The Antelope chief, Lomatowa, was absent at the time of my visit, and did not return for several hours, during which I made several visits to the Snake kiva, returning now and then to see the chief when he came back.

THE ANTELOPE ALTAR

The altar of the Antelope priesthood at Cipaulovi (plate LXXI) was the simplest yet reported in any Antelope kiva, but in form and design was closely allied to that at Walpi. The sand picture was large, measuring 4 by 3½ feet, that at Walpi being only about 32 inches square. The kiva was relatively so small, or the sand picture so near the middle of the floor, that one could see it from outside the room by looking through the hatchway. The border, like that of the Walpi altar, was composed of four bands of sand, colored yellow, green, red, and white, respectively, separated by black lines, as in the Antelope sand picture at Walpi. This border inclosed a rectangular field on which were depicted, in different colored sands, the semicircular rainclouds; four yellow, adjacent to the border; three whole and two half semicircles of green; four red, and three whole and two half semicircles in white. All of these were outlined with black lines. On the remaining part of the inclosed rectangle, which was covered with white sand, there were four zigzag figures with triangular heads, one yellow, one green, one red, and one white, beginning at the left of the sand picture as one approached it from the ladder. Each of these figures had a single black mark on the neck representing a necklace, and a curved horn on the left side of the head, and was outlined in black. In the existence of horns on these zigzag figures they differ from the sand picture at Walpi, where two have horns and the other two squares, the former representing males and the latter females. The black dots for eyes were seen in all these symbols of lightning, but the small nakwakwoci were not put on their necks, and the amulets and cylinders were not observed on the side of the head, as at Walpi. The row of parallel black lines from the semicircles, representing falling rain, were shorter and more numerous than on the Walpi altar.

At each angle of the sand picture there were conical bodies a few inches high, probably of clay, painted yellow, green, red, and white,

---

[1] "Sixth," or "first day" of the second series. It will thus be seen that with the exception of the four snake kuati serious rites were abbreviated in the Antelope kiva.

The pahola or shrine on the plaza

The na

THE SNAKE DANCE AT CIPAULOVI

of meal on a layer of valley sand, which had been evenly sprinkled on the roof of the kiva. When I entered the Antelope kiva, I found eleven priests assembled there, all engaged in making pahos and all with red feathers in their hair. Traces of meal, which had been sprinkled by the priests, were seen on the colored sands of the altar; this was probably an evidence that songs had been sung about it the night before, as I was told had been the case, but was not present.

All the pahos, with certain exceptions to be noted, were of the length of the middle finger, and were painted green, with red points. Each paho was composed of two sticks, one of which, called the female, had a facet at one end. These pahos were tied midway of their length, and to them were attached two herbs, called kunya and sulabe. When I called the attention of the priests to the fact that at Walpi pavanabi was used instead of sulabe, they replied that both were equally efficacious, and had the same intent. In addition to the green pahos, others, painted black, were similarly employed. The pipe-lighter, who, while not the chief, was most communicative, explained the signification of the offerings he made. They were as follows:

1. A black paho.
2. A double-stick green paho or oakwapaho, with six attached nakwakwoci.
3. A green paho with green points.
4. A green paho with black points.
5. Five white-feathered nakwakwocis.

It will be noted that the green pahos were of the length of the middle finger, which is very different from the plumed sticks made by the Antelopes at Walpi on the day before the Snake dance, for on that day the Walpians make a paho the length of the last two joints of the same finger. On interrogating the priests, I discovered that the Walpi rule was not carried out in Cipaulovi, and that there was no variation in the length of the paho.

We have seen how tardy the chief was in making the Antelope altar, and consequently it is apparent why the seven pahos of different lengths could not be made, for the sixteen-song celebration was curtailed in the number of presentations, and its equivalent performed only once or twice.

About noon there were brought into the kiva stalks of corn and vines of the bean, cantaloupe, watermelon, and of certain unknown plants. These were done up with yucca thread in two wads or bundles and placed on the altar, after which the man who tied them together smoked on them for some time and then placed the bundles back of the altar. These bundles were carried in the mouth of the participant in the Antelope dance, which, in Cipaulovi as at the other pueblos, occurred at sunset of this day (totokya).

At the close of the paho making, at about 1.30 p. m., a young man was given a paho, the netted gourd, and an ear of corn. He donned a

W
Y
G
R
B

ALTAR OF THE ANTELOPE PRIESTS AT CIPAULOVI

ceremonial blanket, and was commissioned to deposit the *paho* in a spring. As no songs were sung, and as he bore an ear of corn and a single *paho*, one would naturally have regarded this youth as a novice, but such was not the interpretation given me by the assembly. When the youth returned, he carried spring water in the netted gourd, and still held the ear of corn. The chief took these from him and laid the netted gourd on a little pile of sacred meal near the altar. On the corn, which he deposited near by, he sprinkled sacred meal. The chief then took the pipe, lighted by the pipe-lighter, and smoked several puffs into the water, kneeling on the floor before it. He then handed the pipe to the young courier, who squatted at his side and smoked in turn.

While this was going on, another young man, who had brought into the kiva a number of willow sticks as thick as a lead pencil and perhaps two feet long, began cutting them into small sections, allowing them to fall into a basket tray. After having made these sections, he moistened them and carried the basket out of the room, placing it on the roof of the kiva, so that the moistened twigs might dry in the sun. Later, several balls of clay, about the size of baseballs, were made and placed in the same basket. These are the objects called the "frog's young," which I have described in my accounts of the Snake and Flute ceremonials at Walpi. The Antelope chief then took a flag leaf, moistened it, and made an amulet, rolling the leaf back and forth, in and out, and when finished he tied to it two small feathers. In all respects this amulet was like that carried by the Flute girls in the Flute ceremony or placed on the heads of the female lightning figures on the sand picture of the Antelope altar at Walpi. It was painted black, and one of the netted gourds was placed upon it by the side of the altar.

By this time, or about 2 oclock, all the Antelope priests had finished making their *pahos*, and laid them down, each depositing his prayer-sticks in his own basket tray, in front of the altar, as shown in plate LXXI.

The chief carefully swept the floor of the kiva, gathering up all shavings, whittlings, and fragments of herbs. This refuse was placed in a blanket, sprinkled with meal, and carried out. Shortly afterward a priest brought in all the Antelope rattles and deposited them in the corner of the kiva; all these objects are in his keeping, but each priest brought to the room all his other paraphernalia.

THE ANTELOPE DANCE

The Antelope dance at Cipaulovi took place in the larger plaza at 6.20 p. m. on August 23. A *kisi* was erected on the southern part of this open space, about halfway between the central *pahoki*, or shrine, and the arcades through which the priests came from their kivas. A plank, with a hole in it symbolizing the *sipapu*, was let into the ground immediately before the *kisi*, the entrance to which was closed with a blanket (?) or cloth.

Eleven Antelope and thirteen Snake priests took part in the Antelope dance, and at Cipaulovi, as at Walpi, the whole afternoon was consumed by them in their kivas, costuming for the public exhibition. Shortly before the priests emerged from their rooms, the Antelope chief went over to the Snake kiva, and, without ceremony, asked the Snake chief if he were ready. This was in marked contrast to the formal invitation presented at Walpi, where the Antelope priests sprinkle pinches of sacred meal in the hatchway of the Snake kiva and form a line before it.

Shortly after the return of the Antelope chief to his kiva, the eleven Antelope priests filed out of their secret room, led by their chief. They wore practically the same costume as the Antelopes of Walpi, which seems to be prescribed in all the villages.

The chief carried his *tiponi* across his left arm, and bore in one hand the bow with red horsehair attached to the string. Next to him was a man with the netted gourd, an ear of corn, and a *paho*. There was a third, who later took a position midway in the line and carried a well-filled medicine bowl. Each Antelope wore a ceremonial kilt of white cotton with embroidered ends, ornamented with raincloud symbols in red and dark green. Their faces had a line of white from the corners of the mouth to the ears, and the chin was painted black. They had zigzag lines of white on the breast, arms, and legs; fox-skins depended from their waists behind, turtle-shells were fastened back of the knee, and each was richly ornamented with shell and turquois necklaces. Every Antelope except the chief and the bearer of the medicine bowl carried two rattles. A few of the participants wore cottonwood leaves in their armlets.

The procession, headed by their chief, filed four times around the plaza, the circuit being sinistral, or with the center on the left hand, but not including the *pahoki*. As the Antelopes passed the shrine they threw a pinch of meal toward it, and as they approached the *kisi* each man dropped a pinch of sacred meal on the plank, and stamped violently upon it. At the end of the fourth circuit they formed a platoon, separated into two sections by the *kisi*, the chief standing at the extreme right. They continued shaking their rattles, but not singing, while the Snake priests made their entrance. No *katcinka*, with a whizzer, followed the Antelope priests.

The Snake priests, headed by their chief, came shortly afterward. Their chief carried his bow with red horsehair, but had no *tiponi* or other official insignia. The Snake priests followed him, and the line made four circuits of the plaza, embracing the whole rectangle in their course. As they passed the shrine they dropped a pinch of meal upon it, and when in front of the cottonwood bower they did the same, stamping violently on the plank in the ground.

As a rule the Snake priests were appareled similarly to those of Walpi, but the whole face was painted black, with white under the chin and on the neck. Their cheeks were not smeared with the micaceous hematite which gives such a hideous appearance to the Walpi performers.

After the thirteen Snake men had lined up before the eleven Antelopes, who all the time were shaking their rattles, a low song began, the Antelopes being the singers. As the song progressed the Snake men locked arms and stepped backward and forward, while two men, an Antelope and a Snake, ambled backward and forward between the lines of swaying priests. They went to the *kisi* or cottonwood bower and returned to the head of the lines several times. The Antelope priest then took from the *kisi* the wad of cornstalks and vines and put it in his mouth, as the Walpi priests do the snake. The Snake priest accompanied him, placing his left hand on the shoulder of his companion and acting as the "hugger." In this way the two men pranced slowly between the lines of swaying priests, who stepped forward and backward one step, the Antelopes singing and shaking their rattles. The carrier held the wad in his mouth like a pipe, and after a few courses he was relieved by another priest. After this was continued several times, the wad was returned to the *kisi*, the asperger sprinkled water, and the Snake and Antelope priests filed away in turn, each making circuits of the plaza. No warrior with a whizzer accompanied the procession, and although one of the Antelopes wore a garland of cottonwood leaves, he did not call out at the *kisi* the foreign words, "*Tcamahia, asnahia*," etc.

THE SNAKE RACE

On the morning of August 23, before daybreak, the Antelope priests sang their songs and consecrated the trays of *pahos* before the altar. I regret to record that I was too late to see this ceremony, although I reached the kiva before sunrise. There is every probability that the songs rendered at that time correspond with the sixteen songs, with dramatic accompaniment, which I have observed at Walpi, but as *pahos* were not made in numbers on previous days, it is not probable that a similar ceremony occurred on the other mornings.

When I arrived at the pueblo from my camp near the spring, the "Snake race" was already taking place in the valley between Cipaulovi and Cuñopavi, and all the Antelope priests were seated on the rocky ledge west of the kiva watching for the return of the racers. The race was well attended, many young men from Micoñinovi and Cipaulovi contending, and its termination was clearly visible from the mesa top. It presented no important differences from the Snake race at the other villages; the winner ran up the trail past the Antelope kiva, and the prize seemed to be simply the reputation which it gave him as a runner.

Directly after the return of the racers, a number of boys and girls, who had been standing on the edge of the lower terrace, where lies the trail along which the racers approached the pueblo, started all together to run up the hill to the town. They carried cornstalks, melons, and other objects, and many of them wore small ceremonial kilts and had their bodies decorated with various pigments. As they approached the houses men and women from the spectators ran down to meet them, and, when possible, seized the objects which the children bore. This afforded much pleasure and amusement, and closely resembled what has elsewhere been described in connection with similar races.

Directly after them came a man personating a warrior. He wore a white kilt and an antelope skin, and at intervals twirled a bullroarer or whizzer. He, unlike the winner in the race, returned to the kiva accompanied by all the other Antelope priests. They sat in a circle about the fireplace, smoking and exchanging terms of relationship. After all had smoked, beginning with the chief and ending with the pipe-lighter, each man took a pinch of ashes in his hand and remained silent, squatting on the floor. One of their number sang in a low tone, and as it continued each man turned his hand about his head several times in a circular pass, spat on the ashes, which he then cast out of the hatch. Immediately afterward a bundle of dried roots was passed about, each priest nibbling a little thereof, after which he spat on his hands and rubbed them over his chest. This ceremony was purificatory in nature.

Many pahos were still in the basket trays, and when the winning racer approached, the Antelope chief came out of the kiva and presented one of these to him. At the termination of the race, the warrior[1] bearing the crook deposited the feather, which he wore in his hair, on the Antelope altar.

THE SNAKE DANCE

The Snake dance at Cipaulovi, as in all the other Tusayan pueblos, took place just before sunset; it was well attended by people from the other villages, and included the four Americans in my party. The dance itself was almost identical with that at Walpi, although much smaller in the number of participants.

There were fifteen Antelope and thirteen Snake priests. When the time arrived for the dance, the chief of the Antelopes, who had been dressing in their kiva, went to the hatch of the Snake kiva and asked the Snake chief if he were ready. Immediately after his return, the Antelope-priests filed out of their chamber into the plaza where the kisi had been erected. Their chief carried his badge of office, or tiponi, and he was followed by a priest holding in both hands a medicine bowl and aspergill. This man, however, did not, as in other Snake dances, wear a garland of cottonwood leaves, nor did he cry out the mystic words, "Tcamahia," etc., which formed such a conspicuous feature in the Walpi ceremony. There was likewise no personification of a warrior (Kalektaka) bearing the whizzer or bullroarer.

---

[1] This was the man who stood at one of the goals in the race.

The Antelope priests made four circuits of the plaza, in the space to the southward and eastward of the shrine and kisi, shaking their rattles as they marched, and dropping a pinch of sacred meal in the shrine as they passed it. Each man stamped on the plank before the kisi, dropping meal as he did so, and then the whole line formed a platoon facing eastward, where they stood shaking their rattles.

Immediately the Snake men followed, making four circuits of the plaza, their course being much longer than that of the Antelope priests. As each priest passed before the kisi in these circuits, he stamped on the plank, after having dropped upon it a pinch of sacred meal. They then lined up in front of the Antelope priests, and sang songs similar to those at Walpi. There was no call, however, to the warrior gods by an asperger. Among other episodes at Cipanlovi, I missed that quivering movement of the snake whips, elsewhere described.

The line of Snake men next divided into groups of three—each trio composed of a "carrier," a "hugger," and a "gatherer." The carrier knelt down before the kisi, received a snake from a man within, put it in his mouth, and began the circuit of the plaza. He did not close his eyes, as do the performers at Walpi, and the hugger simply placed one hand on his shoulder. The carrier did not touch the snake, as at Oraibi, after he had placed it in his mouth; and, instead of throwing the reptile from him when he had completed the circuit, he took it out of his mouth and laid it on the ground at a certain place. The gatherer picked up the snake, not confining his attention to the carrier whom he followed, and not first throwing meal to the sun or sprinkling it on the reptile, as at Oraibi. As the carrier started on his circuit, he tucked his paho in his belt. The pahos used at Walpi were made by the Snake priests; those employed at Cipaulovi were made by the Antelope chief and given to the Snake men.

As the snake carrier left the kisi, in his circuit, the asperger sprinkled him with medicine, but no maidens stood near to throw prayer-meal upon them, as at Walpi. After all the snakes had been carried in the mouths of participants in the dance, the Snake chief made a circle of sacred meal about 20 feet in diameter in front of the pahoki, and drew in it six meal radii, corresponding to the six cardinal points. The reptiles were then thrown into this ring, and the asperger sprinkled them with medicine, after which the maidens and women threw sacred meal from their basket plaques upon the writhing mass. At a signal the Snake priests rushed to the reptiles, seized as many as they could, and, as at Walpi, departed hastily down the mesa trails and distributed them to the cardinal points. As they left the plaza, a perfect rain of spittle from the spectators on the surrounding housetops followed them.

The subsequent vomiting and feast differed in no essential particulars from the same episodes at Walpi.

There were among the spectators numerous prominent Snake men from Walpi, including Kopeli the Snake chief, Supela his father, and Saliko his mother. The former did not enter the kivas; and the last mentioned, who came to Cipaulovi the night before the dance, told us she prepared the "antidots" for the priests at Cipaulovi, as at Walpi. In essentials the public Snake dance in the pueblos last mentioned is similar, and the dress of the Snake and Antelope men practically identical. It would seem as if the ceremony were derived from Walpi rather than from Cañopavi.

The Snake dance at Cipaulovi, as will be seen from the foregoing account, is abbreviated in character, small in number of participants, and curtailed in secret rites. On August 21 (Yemoñtotokya), the day before the Antelope dance, the chief went off in search of wood, leaving his altar for a long time, with no one in the kiva for several hours. Such a proceeding may be more primitive, but it never happens at Walpi. While at Walpi the sand picture and altar of the Antelopes are prepared on the first day (yuñya), they are not made until the sixth or seventh day at Cipaulovi, or, more accurately speaking, the third day before the Snake dance. This in itself introduces a modification in secret ceremonials. The awata natci, or bows with red horsehair, were not hung upon the ladders before the eighth day, and were first seen on the ninth; at Walpi, they were placed there on the fifth day. All ceremonials with a snake tiponi were obviously omitted, and there are several complicated rites at Walpi which probably are absent in the Snake villages of other Tusayan pueblos.

THE CUÑOPAVI SNAKE CEREMONY

GENERAL REMARKS

The ritual of this Tusayan village is less known than that of any other, not a single Cuñopavi ceremony ever having been described. There is, however, evidence that the complete Tusayan ritual is performed at this pueblo, and its age and isolation leads me to suspect that the modifications are of value from a comparative point of view. It is, therefore, with great pleasure that I am able, in this article, to present the results of the first study of Cuñopavi ceremonials. Unfortunately, however, I can speak only of the public Snake dance and describe the Antelope altar, since I have not witnessed any of the secret rites pertaining to the ceremony.

The attendance at the Snake dance of Cuñopavi, in 1896, consisted of ten white persons and numerous Indians from the other mesas, in addition to the inhabitants; there were also two Navahos, who had come from a long distance.

THE ANTELOPE ALTAR

The sand mosaic of the Cuñopavi Antelope altar (plate LXXII) was bordered by a margin of sand of four colors—yellow, green, red, and white, separated by black lines—and was of rectangular shape, about the size of the Walpi altar. There were but two rows of semicircular rain-cloud figures in the inclosure of the margin. The first row, adjacent the margin, had four members—yellow, green, red, and white, in sequence, beginning at the right of the row. The second series had five semi-circles—yellow, black, yellow, green, and yellow, following the same sequence as the former. There were four zigzag lightning symbols, colored yellow, green, red, and white, each of which had a horn on the right side of the head. At the angles of each lightning symbol there were drawn, with black sand, figures of feathers. The zigzag lightning strokes and the semicircular rain clouds were outlined with black lines, and parallel lines representing falling rain were short and numerous. As at Cipaulovi, there were no stone implements around the margin of the sand picture, but at its four corners there were small cones of clay, each bearing the color of a cardinal point—yellow, green, red, and white, respectively. The front and rear margins of the sand picture, like those of the Cipaulovi altar, were destitute of objects. On each side of the sand picture there were four clay pedestals, two of which bore straight

sticks and two supported sticks crooked at the extremities. The *tiponi*
was placed on a small hillock of sand somewhat back of the rear right-
hand corner of the sand picture. In the rear of the left-hand corner,
leaning against the wall of the kiva, were two rectangular slabs, the
symbolism on which was not distinct, recalling the so-called Butterfly
virgin slab of the Walpi Antelope altar. Around them were tied
strings with appended *nakwakwoci*.

At the time I studied the Cuñopavi altar of the Antelopes there
were finger marks on each rain cloud of the sand picture, where the
chief had taken a pinch of each colored sand to carry to his field, these
being symbolic of the different colored corn which he hoped would
grow there.

THE SNAKE DANCE

The Snake dance at the pueblo of Cuñopavi was performed on August
24, and was the only event of this complicated observance which I witnessed. While, therefore, my observations were limited, they consti-
tute the first ever made by an ethnologist in this interesting and little
known pueblo. Seventeen Antelope and eighteen Snake priests partic-
ipated in the ceremony; each Antelope carried two[1] rattles, one in each
hand, and there were three small boys among the Antelope priests,
one of whom could not have been more than five years of age. The
youngest of the lads was naked, but painted like his elders, and when
he lined up with the other Antelopes before the *kisi* he held his place
without shrinking, even when the venomous rattlesnakes crawled near
him, an exhibition of infantile pluck which I have never seen excelled.
This is not simply want of fear through ignorance, for again and again
in their songs and talks the priests pray that they may not be bitten.
He must have known the power of the snakes, but the same belief
which controlled his elders gave him courage. The Cuñopavi priests
handled the rattlesnakes more fearlessly, if that were possible, than
the participants at any of the other pueblos.

The differences noted between the events and paraphernalia of the
Antelope and Snake men at Cuñopavi and the other villages were the
following: In addition to cottonwood boughs the *kisi* had cornstalks
in its construction and a circle of sacred meal was made about it.
The costumes and body painting of the Antelopes were the same as at
Walpi; there was no warrior with a whizzer or bullroarer, and the
asperger did not call out the invocation to the cardinal points. The
kilts of the Snake priests were as a rule without rattles, and the parallel lines with which the zigzag figure of the plumed snake were
marked extended across the figure. The bandolier was cylindrical, the
medicine pellets few or wanting.

---

[1] This is an interesting item at Cuñopavi. At Walpi and Oraibi each priest carries but one
rattle. These rattles are made of buckskin stretched over a pair of circular disks and fastened to a
wooden handle; they contain small objects for rattles, and are painted white.

ALTAR OF THE ANTELOPE PRIESTS AT CUÑOPAVI

After the entrance of the Snake and Antelope men and their prelimiary songs, which resembled those of Walpi, the Snake chief went inside the *kisi* and passed out the snakes. Before carrying these reptiles, the Snake priests made the circuit of the plaza in trios, the carrier, hugger, and gatherer posing in the same way as when they bear the snakes. This, of course, was subsequent to the four circuits made in line by the Snake priests when they entered the plaza and stamped on the plank before the *kisi*. The snake carrier handled the reptile, as at Walpi, putting it in his mouth, and did not touch it afterward with his hands, as at Oraibi; his eyes were open as at Cipanlovi and Oraibi. The hugger simply placed his hand on the right or left shoulder of the carrier and stood behind him, not putting his arm about the carrier's neck, as at Walpi. After all the snakes had been carried, and while they were in the gatherer's hands, the Snake priests crowded about the entrance to the *kisi*, and something occurred which was not observable to the spectators. The circle of meal was next made some distance away; the reptiles were then thrown within it, and the women sprinkled or threw their plaques full of meal upon the snakes. The priests then rushed in, seized the reptiles, and darted away, as elsewhere described. As they left the plaza all of the spectators spat after them, as at Cipanlovi. Then occurred something which had never before been witnessed in any of the six presentations of the Snake dance which I have observed. Several of the Snake priests did not obtain reptiles from the writhing mass in the ring of meal, and consequently did not rush down the steep mesa trails with those who did, but they made the circuit of the plaza four times before the *kisi*, sprinkled meal on the *sipapû* and stamped on the plank, after which they filed off to their kiva. It was not clear to me whether this was accidental or an unusual modification; but I am inclined to think that the number of reptiles was so few that these priests could not obtain any with which to rush down the mesa, and this way of retiring to their kiva is prescribed in such a case.

16 ETH——19

General Remarks

On account of the isolation of the pueblo and the persistent way in which its people have resisted innovations, the presentation of the snake ritual at Oraibi has long been regarded as the most primitive of all the Hopi ceremonials.

In an article[1] on the "Ancient Province of Tusayan," Major Powell partially described an Oraibi ceremony, but too briefly to be identified. So far as I know this was the first account of Tusayan kiva rites. A large oil painting of a Tusayan ceremony and altar has long hung in the pottery court of the National Museum. This painting, I am informed by Major Powell, was made under his direction and represents a scene in a Tusayan kiva. Several priests, apparently engaged in rites about a medicine bowl, are figured, and from the arrangement of the maize of different colors about it I suppose the picture represents the making of charm liquid. The attitude of the priest in the act of blowing smoke into the bowl confirms me in this interpretation.

The representation of the reredos is unlike anything which has been reported from Tusayan. The room has a hatchway, but is unlike any Oraibi kiva which I have seen.

In 1895 I figured and described[2] the altar of one of the Flute societies at Oraibi. Mr H. R. Voth, a resident missionary, has recently given much time to the study of the Oraibi ritual, and has shown me several sketches of highly characteristic altars, accounts of which he intends later to publish. We are, therefore, on the way to a more exact knowledge of the ceremonials, religious paraphernalia, and altars of this interesting pueblo which has so long resisted the efforts of ethnologists.

The Antelope Altar

The Antelope priests at Oraibi were not overgenial to strangers wishing to pry into their secret rites, and the Snake priests positively refused to allow me or any white man, except the missionary, Mr Voth, to enter their kiva.[3] I entered the Antelope kiva uninvited, but my

[1] Scribner's Magazine, Vol. 21, No. 2, New York, December, 1875.

[2] The Oraibi Flute Altar; Journal of American Folklore, Vol. VIII, Oct.–Dec., 1895.

[3] One or two white men told me that they ventured into the Snake kiva when the priests were away and saw nothing there but stone images, probably twins, or the Little War Gods. As the Snake chief at Oraibi has no tiponi, he makes no altar, and the stone image was the tutelary god of warriors, known as the Little Gods of War, Püükoñhoya and Palünhoya.

W
Y
G
R
B

ALTAR OF THE ANTELOPE PRIESTS AT ORAIBI

presence there was not welcome, and most of the half hour which I
spent there was occupied in reasoning with the priests. I succeeded
in making a sketch of their altar, but was several times ordered out,
and was therefore not loth to leave the kiva when I had finished.
There was some little satisfaction in being able to tell the priests of
Oraibi in their own kiva that my studies of Antelope altars in other
pueblos enabled me to interpret about every object which theirs pos-
sessed, since they were so similar. This, however, was not strictly
true as regards all the fetishes, for there were two or three objects on
the Antelope altar at Oraibi which are different from those at Walpi,
Cipaulovi, and Cuñopavi, and beyond my comprehension.

The size of the Antelope altar at Oraibi (plate LXXIII) was about the
same as that of Walpi, and the sand picture almost identical, so that a
description of this portion of it would be a duplication of accounts elsewhere published.[1] The sand picture was surrounded by a yellow, green,
red, and white border of sand. There were semicircular figures of rain
clouds in yellow, green, red, and white, arranged in the same order as
at Walpi, and in like sequence. The four lightning symbols, however,
differed somewhat, all of these having square appendages to the heads,
instead of horns and diagonally marked rectangles. These square
appendages, as nearly as I could make out, were on both sides of the
heads, but accuracy in this minute particular was next to impossible.
There were no stone hoes about the border of the sand picture, as at
Walpi. Along each side was a row of clay pedestals, in each of which
were inserted straight or crooked sticks, to the tops of which were
attached red-stained *nakwakwocis*. They were arranged side by side
and there were no breaks or "gateways," as at Walpi. At the side of
each crook a small notted gourd was placed. At the end of each line of
sticks, one on each side of the altar, there was a head of an antelope,
with horns, nose, and neck. These objects are not found on the Antelope altars of Walpi, Cipaulovi, or Cuñopavi, and are significant
accessories in the secret ceremonials.

The floor in front of the altar had no pedestals with upright sticks,
but upon it was a medicine bowl, the six-directions corn, and an
aspergill.

The rear of the altar was strikingly different from that of any Antelope altar which has been described. There were no stone fetishes of
animals, as at Walpi, and although the two *tiponis* were present, both
of these belonged to the Antelopes. The Snake society at Oraibi, as at
Cipaulovi and Cuñopavi, has no palladium or *tiponi*. These two objects
stood just in the rear of the margin of the sand picture, one on each
side of a square medicine bowl, which occupied the middle and therefore corresponds in position to the mountain-lion fetish on the Walpi
altar. Projecting from the top of the left-hand *tiponi* was an object
which, from my point of observation, resembled a stone implement, but

in other respects the two *tiponis* resembled those of the Walpi altar. *Pakos* were placed upright near each *tiponi*, and from one of these a long string, with feathers tied to the extremity, was stretched across the sand picture.

The medicine bowl back of the altar had three T-shape figures painted upon it, and behind this vessel there were four *pahos* placed upright with strings drawn over the top of the medicine bowl. At the extreme left of the rear of the altar there was an ancient vase with terraced elevations. Back of all the objects at the rear of the altar there was a ridge of sand in which was inserted a row of eagle wing feathers. Between the rows of crooks and the lateral margin of the sand picture long *pakos* were laid lengthwise on the floor. A basket of sacred meal was placed on the floor near the right-hand effigy of an antelope head.

It will be seen from an examination of the details of the Antelope altar of Oraibi and comparison with those of Cipaulovi, Cuñopavi, and Walpi, that it is the most complicated and has several objects not elsewhere duplicated. Moreover, the arrangement of the objects back of the altar is such that it would be quite strange, indeed almost impossible, for the Antelope chief to introduce several of the events which occur in the sixteen-song celebration at Walpi.

THE ANTELOPE DANCE

The Antelope or Corn dance at Oraibi took place at sunset, as in the other villages, but it was not so brilliant a spectacle nor was it performed by so many priests as at Walpi. The Antelope priests, headed by their chief, marched directly from their kiva to the *kisi*, and made four circuits of the plaza, each priest stamping on the depressed plank as he passed before it.

After they had formed a platoon, the Antelope chief drew a line of meal in front of them, and at the extreme end of this line he set his *tiponi* upright on the ground. At one side of this badge, also on the line of meal, the asperger deposited his medicine bowl. Each Antelope then placed the netted gourd and stick which he carried on the ground before him, so that all these objects were arranged in a row before the platoon of Antelope priests.

The Snake men came out of their kiva and made four circuits of the plaza in front of the line of Antelope priests, who shook their rattles as the Snakes passed before them. Each Snake priest dropped a pinch of meal and stamped vigorously on the plank as he passed the *kisi*, and then took his place in line before the platoon of Antelope priests. They were led by their chief, an old man, who, however, had no badge of office on his arm. The Antelope priests wore feathers in their hair and a small white feather on the crown of the head. The asperger was distinguished by a fillet of cottonwood leaves. Their bodies were painted with zigzag lines in white, but all wore heavy shell and turquois necklaces. Each priest, except the asperger, carried a rattle in the right hand and a stick and water gourd in the left.

Entrance and escort of the Antelope priests

Entrance of the Snake priests

THE ANTELOPE DANCE AT ORAIBI

Platoons of Antelope and Snake priests at the opening of the dance

Snake priests shaking their whips

THE ANTELOPE DANCE AT ORAIBI

Line of Antelope priests.

The asperger carrying the load of cornstalks and bean vines.

THE ANTELOPE DANCE AT ORAIBI

The chief bore his tiponi over his left arm. All wore white dance kilts with rain-cloud decorations, and a characteristic sash. Several had bandoliers of yarn over the right shoulder and a hank of wool on the left knee, but none of the Antelope priests wore moccasins and but few had fox-skins dangling from their belts. The position of the chief was at the extreme right of the line. An old Antelope priest carried on one of corn.

Each of the Snake priests wore a small red feather in his hair, but their faces were not painted; all, however, had daubs of white pigment on their arms and legs. Several had hastily tied white kilts, similar to those of the Antelopes, about their loins, and only two had the characteristic snake kilts. Each carried his snake whip in his right hand, a bag of meal in his left, and most of the performers wore moccasins. None had necklaces, fox-skins, or bandoliers. The platoon of Snake men stood some distance from the Antelopes, with a lad on the extreme right. As the Antelopes sang and shook their rattles, the Snake men bent slightly forward, pointing their whips toward the ground, then moving them backward and forward with a waving motion. As the music continued, the asperger, not leaving his position by the side of the Antelope chief, called out in a low voice the words "Tcuwakia," etc, several times.

After he had ceased, he went to the opening of the kisi, and took out one of the bundles of cornstalks, melons, and other vines, put the butt in his mouth, holding the other end in both hands before him. A second priest, putting his left hand on the left shoulder of the asperger, walked behind the carrier, stroking his back with a snake whip. In this way the two made several promenades between the platoons of Snake and Antelope priests, the former singing and shaking their rattles, all with netted gourds and sticks in their left hands. As this proceeding continued the Snake priests stepped backward and forward in line, poising themselves first on one leg and then on the other.

At the conclusion of this dance the Snake priests filed about the plaza, making the circuits before the kisi, and returned to their kiva. The Antelope priests did the same, but went to their own ceremonial chamber. This closed totokya (August 18), so far as public ceremonies were concerned.

THE SNAKE RACE

A snake race of Oraibi took place at sunrise of the same day on which the Snake dance was celebrated, as at Walpi, Cipaulovi, and Cuñopavi.

THE SNAKE DANCE

At a short time before sunset, on August 19, the Antelope priests filed out of their kiva and made four circuits in front of the kisi, each stamping on the plank and dropping a pinch of meal as he passed. They were headed by the chief, who carried his tiponi on his left forearm. The chief in turn was followed by the asperger, who wore a

chaplet of cottonwood leaves and carried a medicine bowl and aspergill
with both hands. Each Antelope wore a white "breath-feather" in his
hair, which hung down his back, but none had a bunch of feathers on
his head. The chin was painted black and there was a white line along
the upper border of the black from ear to ear across the upper lip. All
wore necklaces of shell or turquois and each was adorned with zigzag
lines of white pigment along the body, on each breast, from shoulder
to belt, continued on the back on each side to the waist. There were
also zigzag white lines on the arm, and the forearm was painted white.
Each wore a bandolier of woolen yarn over the right shoulder, and
everyone, save the asperger, carried a rattle in the right hand. All
the dancers wore kilts and embroidered sashes, with pendent fox-skins
behind, and all had moccasins. Thus appareled they lined up in a
platoon, the chief at the left, the kisi midway in the line, shaking
their rattles while awaiting the Snake priests.

The Snake priests then came from their kiva headed by their chief,
who had no tiponi. Each Snake priest wore a bunch of feathers in his
hair, and curious feathered objects on the back of the head. Their
faces were blackened, but there was no white paint on the chin. All
wore shell and turquois necklaces, armlets, and wristlets, and daubs of
white on their foreheads, breasts and backs.

Their kilts were colored red, with zigzag figures of the plumed snake,
bearing tripod-shape and alternate parallel bars as ornaments. Less
than half their number had a fringe of antelope hoofs on the lower edge
of the kilt; all wore fox-skins pendent from their loins, turtle-shell
rattles on the leg, moccasins stained red with sesquioxide of iron, and
red wristlets. Each carried a snake whip. After the preliminary
forward and backward steps, and after shaking their whips in unison
with the songs of the Antelopes, they divided into groups of three,
called carrier, hugger, and gatherer.

The snakes are carried at Oraibi in a way peculiar to this pueblo and
differently from that adopted in any other Tusayan village. The posture
of the hugger is likewise exceptional. When the carrier approaches the
kisi in which the snakes are confined, he places his whip in his belt, seizes
the reptile, puts its neck in his mouth, with head pointing to his left,
and grasps the body of the snake with his two hands, the right above
the left. The carrier does not close his eyes, and he takes but one reptile
at a time. In this way he ambles about the plaza in a circle, the center
toward his left. When he has completed the circuit, he takes the reptile from his mouth and lays it on the ground, with the head pointing
away from the kisi. The hugger follows the carrier, placing his left
hand on the left shoulder of the carrier, whose back he strokes with
the snake whip. He stands behind the carrier, and not at his side, as
at Walpi. The gatherer picks up the reptiles after they have been
placed on the ground. If the reptile coils for defense, he strives to
make him recoil by movements of the whip; otherwise he takes a little

Entrance of the Antelope priests

Circuit of the Antelope priests before the kisi

THE SNAKE DANCE AT ORAIBI

Antelope priests in front of the Snake priests at the kisa

Preliminary circuit of the Snake priests in the Antelope dance

THE SNAKE DANCE AT ORAIBI

The dance before the reptiles are taken, from the hut

The snake catch and the troggers

THE SNAKE DANCE AT ORAIBI

sacred meal, says a prayer, casts a pinch to the setting sun, sprinkles a little on the head of the reptile, and suddenly grasps the snake back of the head. The gatherers collect the snakes whenever dropped by the carriers, and hold them in their hands as the others are borne about the plaza.

The women did not stand in line and sprinkle the Snake priests with meal as they passed with their burdens, but when the reptiles were thrown in a heap, after the dance, both maids and matrons emptied trays of meal upon the snakes on the ground.

After all the reptiles had been carried about the plaza in the way indicated above, they were thrown in the middle of a ring of sacred meal, marked with six radii, also of meal, corresponding to the cardinal points, the zenith, and the nadir. At a signal the Snake priests rushed to the circle, seized all the snakes they could gather, and darted off with them down the mesa sides to the four quarters, where the reptiles were deposited. Later they returned, divested themselves of their scanty clothing, retired to a secluded spot, bathed, took an emetic (?), and vomited. The Antelopes meanwhile made four circuits in front of the kisi and retired to their kiva. As at Walpi, the Snake men feasted at nightfall, not having tasted food on the day of the dance.

In reviewing the details of the Snake dance at Oraibi, as described above, we are impressed, first, with the small number of participants, eleven Antelope and fifteen Snake priests; secondly, with the peculiar manner of carrying the reptiles; and, thirdly, with the lack of brilliancy in the personal adornment of the performers. The entrance of the Snake chief, Kopeli, at Walpi, followed by his band, is a most striking affair, full of life and startling in character. At Oraibi this part is very tame in comparison, without dash or excitement, and fails in vigor, energy, and power. The number of participants at Oraibi, not a third of those at Walpi, is also disappointing to one who has seen the dance at the East Mesa. I can, however, well believe that the Oraibi Snake dance more closely resembles that of Walpi before the advent of so many visitors, than does the present exhibition at the latter pueblo. Everything at Walpi shows a vigorous cult, a popular society, an earnestness as great as at Oraibi, but the primitive character of the whole is somewhat spoiled by the introduction of gaudy ribbons, ornaments, and personal decorations purchased from the trader.

DIFFERENCES IN ACCESSORIES

GENERAL REMARKS

The most striking differences in such events as were witnessed in the Snake dance presentations thus far recorded have been noted in the preceding pages. None of them are of sufficient importance to indicate more than local modifications. The strong likenesses which one ceremony bears to the other indicate the same cult and a common origin.

It would, I believe, be a little short of puerile to ascribe the Snake ceremonials in the different Tusayan pueblos to independent evolutions, so close are their similarities in details and so definite are the legends of their common origin. There is, however, an aspect of the study of Snake dances among other pueblos which merits more serious attention, to the intelligent discussion of which exact data on the Tusayan variants may be of value. From a study of the amount of variation in the same rite in these five pueblos, we may obtain a knowledge of the limits of variants which will be of service in comparative studies.

The following are some of the features in the Snake ceremonies which, I am told, did not occur at Oraibi[1] and Cipaulovi:

I. The singing of a series of sixteen songs on the first four days.

II. The personification of the bear and puma, and accompanying rites.

III. Ceremonial mixing of Snake medicine.

As there was no Snake altar at Oraibi, Cipaulovi, or Cuñopavi, the reptiles were not thrown across the room, but simply dried on the sand, as at Sin.

Both at Oraibi and Cipaulovi, pakos of different lengths corresponding to different days and distance of shrines were not made, and as this is a prominent feature in the Walpi variant, its absence has profoundly modified the attendant rites at the other villages, imparting to them many modifications.

PAHOS

Most of the pahos or prayer-sticks made at Cipaulovi on the day before the Snake dance were of the length of the middle finger, while at Walpi they are of the length of the ultimate joint. One of the component sticks has a flat facet, whereas at Walpi neither has a face. The stick with a facet upon it is the female; the other, the male.

[1] Mr H. R. Voth has made elaborate studies of the secret rites of the Oraibi Snake dance, from beginning to end. His observations, when published, will no doubt throw a flood of light on the unknown portions of the ceremonial.

The Dance performance

The Capulinejo entrance

SNAKE PRIESTS WITH REPTILES

Of all the suggestions that have been offered to explain the *paho* on comparative grounds, none seem to me more worthy of acceptance than that it is a sacrifice by symbolic substitute. The folktales of the Pueblos are not without reference to human sacrifice, and offerings of corn or meal would be natural among an agricultural people like the Hopi. Substitutes for human sacrifices to the gods were sometimes made by the Aztecs in the form of dough images, so that the method by substitution, common in Europe, was not unknown in America. When occasion demanded, the Hopi legend says, they sacrificed a child and their chief, but in these days sacrifice has come to be a symbolic substitute of products of the field—corn, flour, or *paho*—still retaining, however, the names "male" and "female," and with a human face painted on one end of the prayer-stick.

THE KISI

Each of the four pueblos of Tusayan where the Snake dance is celebrated has a *kisi* or bower made of cottonwood boughs, near which the Snake dance is celebrated, and in which the reptiles are confined before they are carried about the plaza. These *kisis* are all very similar in their construction, the only difference which I have detected being the use of cornstalks[1] and reeds with the cottonwood boughs in the Oraibi celebration. All were closed in front by a wagon-sheet or cloth.

The *kisi* at Oraibi is placed in the open space west of the town, that of Cipaulovi in the main plaza, and that of Cuñopavi in the plaza between the westernmost and inner row of houses. The vicinity of the *kisi* to a shrine is peculiar to Cipaulovi.

SNAKE WHIPS

The snake whips of the Middle Mesa pueblos are made of two sticks instead of one, as at Walpi, and in some instances have attached packets of cornhusk, presumably containing prayer-meal, which are absent on the Walpi snake whips. These may thus be regarded as true *pahos* or prayer-sticks. The neat little fringed bags of buckskin, in which the Snake priests of Walpi carry their sacred meal, I did not see at Cipaulovi or Oraibi, where the meal bags were large and coarse.

SNAKE KILTS

The snake kilts vary in no important detail in the different villages, except that they are sometimes made of deer or antelope skin, sometimes of cloth, but are always stained red. The zigzag figure in the middle of the kilt is decorated with crossbars alternating with tripod figures or simple parallel lines. The kilts of the Middle Mesa and Oraibi generally have these bars extending across the figure of the

[1] In the Sia variant cornstalks are said to be used in the construction of the "grotto," which Mrs Stevenson describes as "a central structure of cornstalks bearing ripe fruit." This "grotto" I regard as the Sia equivalent of the Tusayan *kisi*.

snake. The lower fringe may be of tin cones or antelope hoofs, or they may be destitute of all appendages, according to the pueblo. Tin cones are universal at Walpi.

The feathers on the heads of the Snake priests vary in the different pueblos, especially those hanging downward on the hair behind. The antelope kilts are similar, and the sashes, fox-skins, and belts identical. The other striking differences have been mentioned in the account of the dance in each pueblo.

The absence at Cipaulovi, Oraibovi, and Oraibi of the personification of the *katcktaka*, or warrior, who carries the bow and arrow, and who twirls the whizzer, is noteworthy. At Walpi this personage appears in the rear of the line of Antelopes as they enter the plaza, then stands at the extreme left of the platoon, and is the last to leave the *kisi* at the close of the dance. He uses the whizzer at critical times in the ceremony, and has appeared in the three Walpi Snake-dances which I have witnessed. He was not, however, seen in any of the villages where this ceremony was celebrated in 1896.

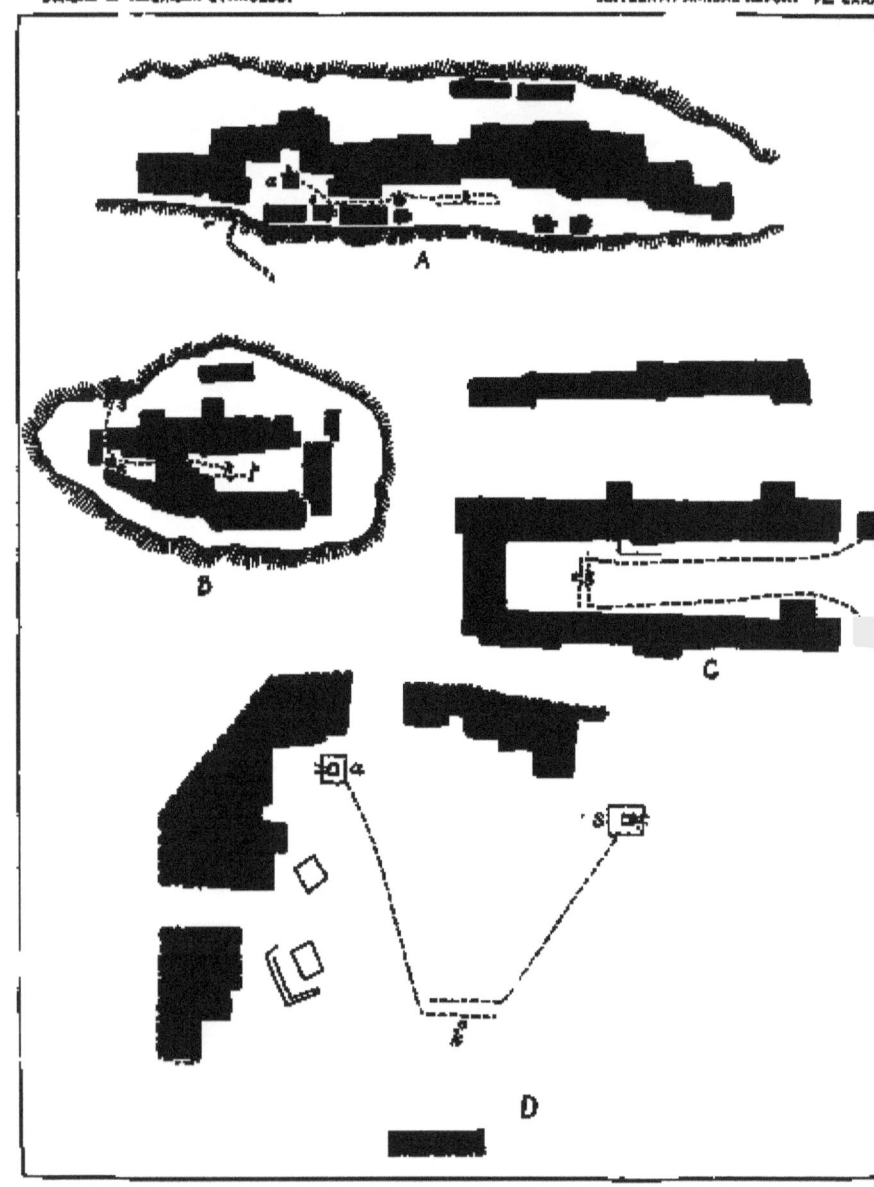

DIAGRAM SHOWING POSITIONS OF KIVAS, KISIS, SHRINES, AND PARTICIPANTS IN THE
SNAKE CEREMONIALS

a, Walpi   b, Cipaulovi   c, Cuñopavi   d, Oraibi

When we attempt to analyze the Tusayan ritual, we are led to suspect that the similarities in the great ceremonials are in part results of composition. The Tusayan people have been made up of increments, which have gradually assimilated, as history and legends describe. Each of these additions brought its own ceremonials, some of which were still practiced, and have been transmitted to descendants, surviving to the present day. The ritual has thus come to be one of composition, not of replacement.

Christianity had a like reception when it came among the pueblos. It was engrafted on the Pagan system, and so long as it was not thought to be aggressive it was welcomed; but so soon as the new cult sought to replace existing rites, it encountered resistance. Each priesthood held that its rites were efficacious, and those of associate societies were likewise good; but when any one of these priesthoods declared those of another bad, a position which to their minds was illogical, since the priests of one fraternity do not know the secret rites of another, an unusual condition arose. As history shows, there was no objection to Christianity at its advent, and it took its place with numerous Tusayan cults, in their system; but the attempt to overthrow the latter led to the hostilities which culminated in 1700.

The several components which formed the Tusayan people practiced ceremonials similar in general character, but different in details. As they became united, each retained certain of its ceremonials, which have been transmitted to our time. The similarities we detect show how close these components were.

The comparative studies of the Snake presentation which I have made in the three pueblos that celebrate this drama in the even years have led me to the conclusion that in my previous publications sufficient emphasis has not been placed on the corn worship which runs through it. The recognition of this element I owe more especially to studies of the Flute ceremonials, which, as I have insisted, are in many respects akin to the Snake dances.

As will be seen by a study of the altars of the Antelope priests, they are destitute of any idol, so that no clew can be obtained from that source in regard to the deity addressed. There are in each, however, figures of rain clouds, which prove, so far as they go, the correctness of the belief that rain worship is at least one of the most prominent features. The fetish of the War god in the Snake kiva of Oraibi is

evidently a special feature as a guardian of warriors, and of small significance in a broad discussion of the meaning of the Snake dance.

Looking over the participants in the secret ceremonials of the Antelope kiva of Walpi, there are but two celebrants whom we can identify
as personators. The Antelope priests, save possibly their chief, are
simply celebrants, but the boy and girl who stand in the corners of the
kiva must be something more; they represent some personage, and
consequently I have reflected on their identity. The names given me
for these two children are the Snake-youth and the Snake-maid. These
names are, I believe, simply cultus-hero names applied to them because
of the societies which celebrate the rites. Who the Snake-boy really
is I am not yet prepared to say, but I think the Snake-maid is simply a
personation of the Corn-maid, and these are my reasons for that belief:

A supernatural being or mythological conception may be represented
by Hopi priests in several ways. There are three methods which occur
to me—(1) a symbolic picture, (2) an image, and (3) a personification by
a man, woman, or child. Designs on the reredos of altars, sand mosaics,
altar slabs, and the like, are examples of the first. The rain clouds on
the Antelope sand picture, the painted sun disks in the *Palülükonti*
screen drama, are symbolic of the supernaturals which they represent.
Images likewise represent certain gods; but they are not the gods, only
symbols in graven forms, as figures are symbolic pictures. The third
and highest form are personifications by men, women, or children.
When necessity compels, or for practical reasons, these personifications
are simply represented by symbols, effigies, or idols. Instead of a man
representing the sun, we have a painted disk. This is carried out in
different presentations of the same ceremony accordingly as it is elaborated or abbreviated. Thus, in one presentation of the *Humiskatci* a
woman was dressed like a certain goddess, but in another this personification was replaced by a picture of this supernatural on a board;
both had the same name, both the same intent. Practical reasons led
to a personification in one and a symbolic picture in the other presentation of the ceremony.

Bearing this thought in mind, let us return to a study of the Snake-
maiden. When we compare her with other personifications in the
Tusayan ritual, we find she is clothed in precisely the same manner,
wears the same symbols, and in every way is identical with the girls in
the Flute ceremony; she is, in fact, the same personage. Our studies,
therefore, naturally lead us to ask who the girls of the Flute ceremony
represent. We have more to guide us in this search.

The girls in the Flute are called the *Lenya-manas*, or Flute-maids, a
name applied also to certain figurines on the Flute altars. This name
is likewise a sacerdotal totem name of cultus heroes or tutelary deities
of a Flute society.

The images of the Flute-maids on the altar represent the Corn or
Germ maids. Of that there is proof, because they are sometimes

called by that name and they have figures of corn painted on their bodies. Images of the same, highly elaborated into dolls, are known by the secular name, *Calako* (Corn) maids. These dolls have characteristic symbols on the cheeks, the same rain-cloud ornaments on the head, a figure of an ear of corn on the forehead, eyes of different color, and painted chins. A *Calako-mana* is the same as the effigy of the Flute-maid on the Flute altar, only with another name. In the *Lalakonti* she is called the *Lakone*-maid, and in the *Mamzrauti* the *Mamzrau*-maid, indicative of the society on whose altars they stand, just as the *Leuya*-maid in the *Leuya* or Flute society. All are special names of the same personage, the Corn-maid, *Hüiyiwü*, the Mother of Germs.

In the secret ceremonials of the Flute it is not practicable to have a personification of the Corn-maid standing for nine days and nights near the altar, and she is therefore represented by an effigy, which is the image spoken of. But it is not desirable that the uninitiated should see this image, consequently it is not brought out on the plaza in public ceremonials. For this reason, at that time the girls personify the Corn-maids. Hence the two maids in the Flute ceremonials represent the same supernaturals as the images. They are the Corn-maids of legends, the Germ-girls, the Mothers of Germs, *Hüiyiwü*. If the *Leuya-manas* are the Corn-maids, then *Tcüa-mana*, the Snake virgin, *Lakone-mana*, the Lakone virgin, and *Mamzrau-mana* are the same. The girl in the Antelope dramatization is therefore a Corn-goddess.

Let us see if the theory that the *Tcüa-mana* and the *Leuya-mana* are Corn-goddesses is supported on other grounds.

The Snake-maid in the dramatization[1] holds a bowl, stalks of corn, and bean vines; the Flute girls carry flat wooden slats, called corn *puhos*, on which corn is depicted. The chins of both are blackened, like the image of the *Lakone-mana*, Corn-maid. The entrance of the Flute girls into the town on the ninth day of the Flute ceremony corresponds, according to legends, with the entrance of the Corn-maids. The Snake-maids whom Tiyo is reported to have brought from the underworld, personified by the *Tcüa-mana* in the Antelope rites, wore clouds on her head, as do the images of the Flute maids and the girls who personate the *Lakone-mana* in the public dance. She brought all kinds of corn; so likewise the various others with whom she is identical. The so-called Snake-maid is, therefore, simply one of the Corn-maids, and the dramatization[2] in the Antelope kiva at Walpi is connected with her worship.

In ancient ceremonies we may conjecture that the gods were personified in the kivas by men or women dressed in an appropriate way and bearing prescribed symbols. In course of time, however, for practical or other reasons, images or symbolic pictures were substituted for

[1] Journ. Amer. Eth. and Archaeol., Vol. IV, pp. 60, 76. The corn-stalks and bean vines are carried in the bowl called the *patne*, q. v.

[2] Journ. Amer. Eth. and Archaeol., Vol. IV, pp. 76-81.

personifications. The secret ceremonials of the Antelopes are still in that archaic condition, and the Corn-maid is still represented at Walpi by a girl of the pueblo. In the Flute rites, however, the Germ-maids or Corn-maids are represented in the secret ceremonials by effigies on the altar, and in the public part of the dance by persons—maidens of certain prescribed clans.

In the *Lálakoñti* we have the same images of Corn-maids as on the Flute altars, and personifications of the same by girls in the public dance. In the *Mamzraúti* the conditions are the same as in the *Lálakoñti*.

Were it desirable to extend our comparisons beyond the boundaries of Tusayan to Cibola, we should there find the personifications taken by maids representing the Corn-maids in the *Kiakwey* and *Hampoñey*, as I have elsewhere[1] described.

By a similar course of reasoning by which we have determined the identity of *Tcüa-mana* (Snake virgin), *Lenya-mana* (Flute virgin), *Lakoñ-mana* (Lakoñ-virgin), and *Mamzrü-mana* (Mamzrü-virgin), the associate male or boy, called *Tcüa-tiyo*, *Lenya-tiyo*, *Lakoñ-tiyo*, and *Mamzraú-tiyo* would also appear to be society names of the same personage. In the Walpi Snake-Antelope ceremony he carries a reptile; in the Mishoñinovi Flute altar his effigy bears a flute; in the Walpi *Lálakoñti* he is *Cotokinwüwû*, a Sky god. The only intimation of his identity would seem to be suggested by the last mentioned. He is the renowned cultus hero appearing in different guises in these four ceremonials. In one of the variants of the Snake legend, however, he is called White-corn, an attributal name, no doubt, which varies in the different ceremonials or religious fraternities.

Two variants of the legend of the Snake society have been published which apparently differ very greatly, but which in essentials are similar, although neither of these pretends to be accurate in details. In the variant first referred to,[2] one of seven brothers, named from different colored corn, sought and found a maiden in a cave inhabited by Snake people, under guidance of a snake. These maidens were dancing, and the great snake chief "took hold of a cloudy substance," and began pulling, when a girl, "Bright-eyes," emerged, and was given to him as a wife. Under her direction, "White-corn," the youth, sought his home, and his bride was known as *Tcüawügti*. When they joined his kindred, it was "noticed" (recognized) that in times of drought her prayers for rain were efficacious. The people desired her to erect the rain-cloud altar of her native home, to which she replied, "Not until a child is born." She later conceived (in a tempest), and the people were glad, because they hoped for a rain chief. White-corn and his wife retired to a distant mesa, and after seven days returned with her offspring, seven reptiles. The people sought in their disappointment to

[1] Journ. Amer. Eth. and Archæol., Vol. I, pp. 45-55.

[2] Legend of the Snake order of the Hopi as told by outsiders. Journ. American Folk-lore, Vol. I, 1888. Snake ceremonials at Walpi, Journ. Amer. Eth. and Archæol., Vol. IV, 1894.

kill the brood, but an old man took them with the mother and father to his house. Something of unknown character happened in that house, and the Snake-woman, her offspring, and the old man vanished. The old man came back alone; the Snake-woman never returned. There are many details which I have omitted, but the essentials to which I would call attention are that a young man, after many adventures, found in a cave inhabited by Snake people a maid, whom he brought to the home of his own kin. She gave birth to reptiles and disappeared. The name of the young man was White-corn; the Snake-maid was associated with rain clouds.

The incidents of the second variant are more detailed. I need not mention them, but will restrict my account to the main outline.

A youth, under guidance of Spider-woman, visited the underworld and had many adventures with several mythic beings. He entered a room where people were clothed in snake skins, and was initiated into mysterious ceremonials, in which he learned prayers which bring corn and rain. He received two maids, associated with clouds, who knew the songs and prayers efficacious to bring rains. He carried them to the upper world to his own people. One, the Snake-woman, he married; the other became the bride of the Flute-youth. His wife gave birth to reptiles. He left them and their mother, and migrated to another country.[1]

When we examine the legend of this youth, Tiyo, and his adventures in search of the two maids, we see still other evidences of the germ-worship or corn-worship referred to above. In the Snake kiva of the other world the chief told him, "Here we have abundance of rain and corn; in your land there is but little; so thus shall you use the *nakwá* [charm liquid to bring them]; fasten these prayers in your breast; and these are the songs you shall sing, and these the *pahos* you shall make [for that purpose]; and when you display the white [zigzag lines of kaolin] and the black on your bodies, the clouds will come." When the chief gave Tiyo portions of the different colored sands from the altar, he said, "These are the colors of the corn Tiyo's prayers will bring"—that is, symbols of corn. He gave the two corn-rain maids[2] into Tiyo's keeping—one for himself and one for his younger brother (presumably the Flute chief).

I believe, however, we should not seek to identify too minutely the details of myths or legends in ceremonial proceedings, for undoubtedly the Hopi variants are more or less distorted, changed, and otherwise modified in recital, translation, and transmittal.

The main points are, however, comparable; a cultus hero sought a mythic land blessed with abundance, and brought from that favored place the corn-rain maids, whose worship was powerful in bringing food and rain.

---

[1] Journ. Amer. Eth. and Archæol., Vol. IV, pp. 106-116.

[2] These maids were enveloped by white fleecy clouds; the edges of the Corn-maids have symbols of clouds on their heads.

Stripped of poetic embellishment, the legend has a practical interpretation. The two necessities, corn and rain, failed the ancient Hopi
at some early epoch in their history, so that they were in danger of
starvation, when one of their number, furnished with prayer offerings
as sacrifices, sought other people who knew prayers, songs, and rites to
bring the desired gifts. In order to learn these charms, he was initiated
into their priesthood by this foreign people, and to make that adoption
complete, married one of their maids, and, to save his brethren, he
brought his bride and offspring to live with his own people. Her
children were like those of her family (the Snake clan) and unlike
his, and hence trouble arose between them. The mother returned to
her own land and the father also sought a new home. Their children
inherited the prayers and songs which bring corn and rain, and they
were ancestors of the present Snake people.[1]

So it is, I believe, that every year, when the proper time comes, the
men of the Snake family who have been initiated into the Snake
fraternity, and the descendants to whom these prayers, songs, and
fetishes were transmitted, assemble, and in order that their work may
resemble the ancestral, and thus be more efficacious, they gather the
reptiles from the fields, dance with them as of old, personating their
"mother," the Corn and Mist maids, in the kiva dramatization, and at
the close of the dance say their prayers in hearing of the reptiles that
they may repeat them to higher deities. In other words, they strive to
imitate the conditions, so far as possible, which tradition ascribes to
that favored place of the Snake people, where corn is plentiful and
rain abundant. The worship of a Great Snake plays no part, but the
dance is simply the revival of the worship of the Snake people as
legends declare it to have been practiced when Tiyo was initiated
into its mysteries in the world which he visited.

In the same way we may explain the Flute observance as a ceremony
for the fructification of corn and production of rain. The Flute-youth
also obtained as his bride a Corn-mist maid. Her children were not
serpents, but ancestral members of the Flute clans, and when the
descendants celebrate their dance, representatives of her people take
part.

The nucleus of the Hopi confederacy is said to have been formed by
a consolidation of these two phratries, the Snakes and the Flutes, who
are reputed to be of the same blood, since their mothers were of the
same people. But the mother of the Snake people, Tcüamana, in olden
time gave birth to reptiles, the older brothers of Snake men. Striving
to reproduce the ancestral ceremonials, representatives of the legendary
participants are introduced, and these are the reptiles which are

---

[1] Notwithstanding strong claims are made to the contrary for other societies, I think there is evidence of an intimate relationship between the Snake-priesthood and the Snake phratry, as I have already
elsewhere shown. This conclusion is likewise supported by Hodge's study of the Keresan and
Tanoan clans. There are, of course, many priests in the Snake fraternity at Walpi from other
phratries, but the majority, including the chief, are from the Snake people.

gathered into the kivas. They are washed,[1] because everyone who takes part in a ceremony must first bathe as a purification.

While this theory of the Snake dance is plausible, it offers no explanation of why the reptiles are carried in the mouths of the priests. It can readily be seen that it presupposes that they dance in the plaza with the priests, but why are they not simply carried in the hands? For this I confess I have no adequate explanation, but the fact that they are carried in the hands as well as in the mouths at Oraibi is suggestive, especially if the Oraibi celebration is the most primitive. If we suppose that the Oraibi method is intermediate in development between that of Walpi and the ancestral, we may suppose that formerly the participants danced with the snakes in their hands. Some daring priest, for a sensation, still holding the reptile in this way, put its neck in his mouth, possibly to prevent its coiling and hiding its size. That method was startling and was adopted by all, a condition which persists at Oraibi. A further evolution of the custom would be the removal of the hands, when the reptile would be carried wholly in the mouth, as at Walpi, Cipaulovi, and Cuñipavi.[2]

We have knowledge of pueblo peoples where the custom of carrying reptiles in the hands still persists, or survived to within a few years, but that does not prove that Tusayan derived its dance from that source. The participants in the Keresan Snake dances probably did not carry the reptiles in their mouths. In Espejo's reference to the Acoma variant, in 1583, no mention is made of this startling method of handling reptiles, and it would hardly have escaped mention had it been noticed, as it must have been had it existed. Mrs Stevenson, in her valuable account of the Snake dance of Sia, does not mention the custom of putting the snake in the mouth, but speaks of the Sia priests as carrying them in their hands. The Hopi claim that the Keresan priests never put the reptiles in their mouths. Thus the evidence, such as it is, seems to point to the conclusion that the habit was locally developed in Tusayan.

The public exhibition, called the Antelope dance, on the afternoon of the eighth day, is evidently connected with corn celebrations, for at that time a wad of cornstalks and melon vines, instead of the reptiles, is carried in the mouths of the priests, as on the following day.

The episode in the Snake kiva at Walpi, when the bear and puma personators carried cornstalks in their mouths and moved them before the faces of men, women, and children spectators, has probably the same significance.[3] The pinches of different colored sand which were taken from the sand picture of the Antelopes before it was dismantled were carried to the cornfields, as symbolic of the different colored corn they hoped their prayers would bring conformably to the legend of its efficacy in that direction.

[1] Journ. Amer. Eth. and Archæol. Vol. IV, pp. 45-46.
[2] The same method appears to have existed elsewhere. American Anthropologist, Vol. VI, No. 3, 1893.
[3] Journ. Amer. Eth. and Archæol. Vol. IV, pp. 62, 63.

While this bird element of corn worship and rain ceremonials runs through the whole festival, that part of it which pertains to rain-making is most prominent in the work of the Snake priests, while corn rites pertain to the Antelopes. The two elements are interwoven, but, as would naturally be the case, the corn rites are most prominent in the kiva celebrations of the Antelope priests. The Antelope chief controls the ceremony, and his priests dance with the wad of cornstalks in the Corn dance.[1]

My efforts to discover the identity of the asperger who calls out the Keresan words, "Tcamahia," etc,[2] at the Nai, have not been rewarded with great success. He apparently is not represented at Cipaulovi and Cuñopavi, but is personated at Oraibi and Walpi. He alone wears the coronet of cottonwood, and his body is characteristically decorated. Undoubtedly he is not one of the Antelope priests, for he takes no prominent part in Antelope secret rites. He is not a Snake priest in function or dress. Two facts throw a glimmer of light on his identity. The words which he calls out are Keresan words, and in the legend[3] of the Snake hero, "Tcamahia" is said to have left the Snake people and to have been joined by other clans at the Keresan pueblo, Acoma. In addition there may be quoted the statement of the Antelope chief that a personified representative from Acoma joins them biennially and assists them in the public exhibition of their dance. It seems as if the asperger who utters the Keresan invocation may personate a Keresan visitor, the ancestral wanderer, who left the Snake people in ancient times, and met other people from another direction at Acoma. His dress and speech are different, for he is not a Hopi; he is of the older stock, known by the same name as the ancient stone implements on the Antelope altar, tcamahia, the ancients, whom some of the Hopi claim did not come upon the earth through the same sipapû as themselves, but who at their advent were living in the far east.[4]

I have given much thought to the question why Antelope priests are so called, and what connection there can be between the antelope and the snake in this nomenclature. At one time I even doubted whether I could believe my Hopi friends in their statements that they were Antelope priests, notwithstanding their name, Tcübwympkiya, has the

---

[1] The erroneous statement that the "hugger" in the Snake dance is an Antelope priest is published in many accounts of the Snake dance. This inaccuracy arose from the fact that in the Antelope dance an Antelope priest carried the wad of cornstalks and vines. Throughout the Snake dance all the Antelopes remain in line, singing, and holding such reptiles as are passed to them by the gatherers, but the "hugger" in the Snake dance is always a Snake priest.

[2] Journ. Amer. Eth. and Archæol., Vol. IV, pp. 70, 91.

[3] Op. cit., p. 117.

[4] With our present light it would be little more than plausible speculation to conclude that the Snake dances of the Rio Grande pueblos of Keresan stock originally came from Tusayan. That the Snake dance at Sia is closely alike that in Tusayan there is no doubt, and that Acoma had a Snake dance in 1885 is well known. A colony of Kawaika (Keresan) once lived in Antelope valley of Tusayan, or at least there is a ruin there called by the same name as Laguna, where there was also formerly a Snake dance. The indications are that the Keresan Snake dances are of the same source as those of the Hopi, but Keresan words in the Hopi invocation may admit of a different interpretation.

root of *tebbe*, antelope.[1] A study of the Oraibi altar effectually silences all doubt on that score, for the effigies of antelopes' heads form part of its paraphernalia. I have no satisfactory explanation of the connection of the two priesthoods, but offer this suggestion: The Ala or Horn people, now identified with the Flute, originally lived with the Snake people, possibly as two phratries. When they separated, in an ancestral home, a majority wandered off with the Flute people, but a few remained with the Snakes. The predominating clans gave their names to the two groups, but although a number of the Ala people remained with the Snakes, it was not large. These Ala or Horn people were Antelopes, and their sacerdotal descendants are the Antelope priests; but the clans were small and became extinct, and the chiefs came from the predominating Snake family. The old name of Antelope remained, and their symbol in effigy persists on the Oraibi altar, but the clan was lost for a time.

Among the Flute branch the Ala people were vigorous, and retained both blood and name, so that when Snake and Flute people came together again, in Tusayan, they recognized each other as kin. At that time, indeed, the Horn family existed in Walpi in Akoaka, and he was naturally sent to spy out the character of the Flute men when they came. This personage is still represented in the Flute dance at that pueblo, as I have elsewhere described.[2]

Summing up the foregoing speculations, I am led to state the following probabilities which may be used as suggestions in future attempts to divine the meaning of the Snake dance. That the ceremony is a rain-making observance can not be doubted, and the nature of many acts shows that it is likewise tinged with sun worship. To these must now be added corn or seed germination, growth and maturity, implied in the somewhat misleading name "Corn-dance," a dominating influence in every great rite of Tusayan. I am inclined to believe that the Snake dance has two main purposes, the making of rain and the growth of corn, and renewed research confirms my belief, elsewhere expressed, that ophiolatry has little or nothing to do with it. If there is any worship of the snake, it is of such a nature that it may be more correctly designated ancestor worship. Nor does it appear to me that the snake, as here used, is wholly a symbol of water, as the frog, tadpole, or dragonfly. The reptile is introduced as a totemic personation by the society of the Snake phratry to reproduce ancestral conditions in which the ceremony was performed as the legend indicates. The same thought is expressed in a similar way in widely different Tusayan ceremonies. Take any one of the *katcinas*, for instance; they do not introduce the totemic animal, to be sure, in the *Katcina* dance, but they personate it by wearing masks. They thus attempt to resurrect the

[1] Note likewise the element *tcû* in *Tcûamwûmptkiya*, Snake priest, and *Tcûbwûmptkiya*, Antelope priest.
[2] Journal of American Folk-lore, Vol. VII, No. xxvii, p. 267.

ancient performers or dramatize archaic celebrations. Where the drama induces them to introduce certain mythic animals, practical reasons lead them to personate what they can not obtain. They personate the duck (*Pawik*), and it is believed when they don the mask of *Pawik*, they become *Pawik katcinas*, and thus they perform the ceremony as did their totemic ancestors. Reptiles, however, are easy to obtain; their personation by men is therefore not necessary, and most tenacious of all in its influence, the presence of the snake is a startling component which fascinates and survives.

This theory implies but does not necessitate former belief in totemic descent. Certainly the evidence which we have leads us to believe that the Snake people, with a snake totem, believe they are descended from the Snake-woman, or if they stoutly deny descent from reptiles at present, may have once held it. Their denial, however, is only so much evidence, and is not necessarily decisive proof. White men as well as Indians deny many things which the comparative scientific method demonstrates to be true.

The valuable article by Mrs Stevenson gives us about all that is known of the character of the Snake dance among the Keres. Although Hodge[1] has found evidence that this ceremony was of late introduction in Sia, we may rightly suppose that the celebration described by Mrs Stevenson gives an idea of its general character among Keresan communities. I have already shown the points of similarity of the Snake dance of Walpi and that of Sia, as described by Mrs Stevenson, and have called attention to the probable meaning of these similarities, viz. derivation either from each other or differentiation of both from the same culture. The studies of the three Tusayan variants of the Snake dance, which are described in the preceding pages, add further evidence of relationship between the Tusayan and Keresan Snake dances. As would naturally be suspected, the Sia ceremonial differs more from any one Tusayan variant than the Tusayan dances differ among themselves, but the resemblances of the Oraibi, or most primitive, are closer to that of Sia than the highly differentiated Walpi performance.

The only other theory besides the derivation to account for these similarities of Tusayan and Keresan Snake dances would be that of independent origins, now being vigorously advocated in many quarters. While I am heartily in sympathy with this movement as a protest against wild comparisons and deductions from isolated likenesses of objects or myths, it may be carried too far. Members of the Keresan and Tusayan stocks, if we may so call them, have repeatedly been brought together in historic times. People from the Rio Grande have migrated in a body to Tusayan and built towns there or become assimilated with the sedentary inhabitants of that province. So, likewise, other peoples who once lived in Tusayan have moved back to the Rio Grande, and their descendants now form a component of pueblos like Laguna, Sandia, and others. This fact in itself is indicative of resemblances in ceremonials among these separated peoples, and when in studying the Snake dance of Sia and Tusayan we find many likenesses—not one or two resemblances in symbols and paraphernalia, but many resemblances in minute details—we rationally conclude that they are derivative and not of independent origins, due to a similar mind acted upon by a like environment.

[1] American Anthropologist, April, 1896, p. 131. Introduced by the "Corhiti about more than thirty years ago."

The resemblances between Tusayan and Keresan Snake dances, which become more detailed as we study variants of the former at Oraibi and the Middle Mesa, render it less probable that two ceremonials coinciding in so many particulars originated independently. I hold, however, that we can not yet satisfactorily answer the question whether the Tusayan Snake dances were derived from the Keresan, or vice versa, or whether both differentiated from a common source.

Hodge[1] favors the idea that "the former Laguna Snake rites were introduced from the Hopi rather than from Acoma, where its influence was so slight as to leave not even a traditional trace," and he regards it quite likely that the Snake ceremony performed at Laguna only twenty years ago had its origin among the Hopi, and that it came, not "probably from Oraibi," as the Laguna people say, but more likely from the now ruined pueblo of Kawaika, whose name adhered to the newly founded pueblo near the lagoon. The people of the old "Kawaika" pueblo in Antelope valley came to Tusayan originally from the "far east," probably the Rio Grande. The theory that the Laguna Snake ceremony was derived from those Kawaikas who settled in Tusayan implies, of course, that some of them returned when Laguna was settled, which is possible; but the question whether the Acoma people did not have the Snake dance before western Kawaika was built, or before colonists left the east to settle in Antelope valley, is pertinent. If it had, as I suspect it did, the introduction of the Snake cult in Laguna from Tusayan pertains only to one Keresan locality, and we have yet to show that Acoma derived it from Tusayan. The Keresan songs and invocation in the Tusayan rites admit of but one interpretation. They at least were derived from Keresan sources.

The presentation of the Snake dance and accompanying Snake rites at Oraibi is closer to that of Sia than any of the Tusayan variants, and everything goes to show that it is the most primitive. The Walpi dance, on the other hand, has become more specialized, and is the most unlike the Sia as described by Mrs Stevenson;[2] but the question whether the Tusayan Snake cultus was derived from the Keresan, or vice versa, remains unanswered.

The meaning of the Snake dance can not, I believe, be made out completely without comparative studies, and can not be obtained from living priests. As pointed out by Tylor, in speaking of the religions of the great nations, so in that of Tusayan—

In the long and varied course in which religion has adapted itself to new intellectual and moral conditions, one of the most marked processes has affected time-honored religious customs, whose form has been faithfully and even servilely kept up while their nature has often undergone transformation. . . . The natural difficulty of following these changes has been added to by the sacerdotal tendency to ignore and obliterate traces of the inevitable change of religion from age to age, and to convert into mysteries ancient rites whose real barbaric meaning is too far out of harmony with the spirit of a later time.[3]

[1] Op. cit., p. 135.
[2] Eleventh Annual Report of the Bureau of Ethnology.
[3] Primitive Culture, Vol. II, p. 362.

I have no doubt that at some future time enough material will be collected to enable the ethnologist to give a rational explanation of the meaning of the Snake dance from comparative studies, but I doubt very much whether the Tusayan priests now know its original meaning. The trail for the ethnographer is, however, plain; it is highly essential that renewed efforts be made to record more accurately than has yet been done the unknown details of the Tusayan Snake dance before it is finally abandoned or transformed by modifications.   Whatever current explanations are now regarded as orthodox by the priests should be given weight as evidence, but not regarded as decisive.

Of more than usual interest in a study of the distribution of the Snake ceremonials is the following reference, which I quote without comment:

It was discovered [that] the Cocopahs, like the Moquis of Arizona, practise the Snake Dance ceremony.   Not far from their village is an old adobe house especially constructed for this purpose.   Here they annually resort, to avoid publicity, to have their Snake dance.   Rattlesnakes are taken to this house, where the people of the Snake clan congregate and perform their hazardous ceremony.   (From letter in Chicago Tribune, dated Pomona, Cal., October 31, 1895?)

BAXTER, HUBERT H. The Moqui Snake Dance.

American Antiquarian. Vol. XVII, No. 4, Good Hope, Ill., July, 1895.

BOURKE, JOHN G. The Snake Ceremonials at Walpi.

American Anthropologist, Washington, April, 1895.

COX, CURTIS P. Moqui Snake Dance.

Moqui Mission Messenger, Vol. 1, Nos. 2, 3.

FEWKES, J. WALTER. The Oraibi Flute Altar.

Journal of American Folk-lore, Vol. VII, No. 31, Boston, October-November, 1895. (Notes on Walpi Snake dance of 1895.)

—— A Comparison of Sia and Tusayan Snake Ceremonials.

American Anthropologist, Vol. VIII, No. 2, Washington, April, 1895.

GARLAND, HAMLIN. Among the Moqui Indians.

Harper's Weekly, August 15, 1896, (Illustrated by Langren. (The best popular account of the Walpi Snake dance yet published.)

HOUGH, F. W. Pueblo Snake Ceremonials.

American Anthropologist, Vol. IX, No. 4, April, 1896.

MALLERY, G. Les Indiens Moki et leur danse du serpent.

Nature, Vol. XXIV, Paris, 1896.

POLITZER, J. H. Snake Dance of the Moquis.

Herald, New York, November 12, 1894.

—— Mouthfuls of Rattlesnakes.

Examiner, San Francisco, October 21, 1894.

—— The Moqui Serpent Dance.

Republic, St. Louis, November 7, 1894.

—— Among the Moquis.

Daily Traveller, Boston, November 7, 1894. (Describes Oraibi Snake dance.)

RUSS, H. N. The Moqui Snake Dance.

Land of Sunshine, Los Angeles, January, 1896. (Illustrated account of Walpi Snake Dance of 1895.)

—— Through Arizona's Wonderland.

Inter Ocean, Chicago, July 28, 1896.

STEVENSON, M. C. The Sia.

Eleventh Annual Report of the Bureau of Ethnology, Washington, 1894. (Contains a description of the snake ceremonies of Sia pueblo.)

ANONYMOUS. Snake Dance of the Moqui Indians; a religious drama and a prayer for rain.

Times-Herald, Chicago, October 13, 1895.

—— The Snake Dance.

Journal, Boston, August 29, 1895.

—— A Moqui Snake Dance.

Bulletin, San Francisco, September 3, 1895; Evening Sun, New York, September 14, 1895.

—— Snake Dance of the Moquis.

Herald, New York, November 11, 1894; Bee, Omaha, September 22, 1895.

—— An Indian Snake Dance.

Register, New Haven, September 22, 1895.

—— Walpi Arizona Snake Dance.

Evening Gazette, Boston, October 20, 1894, reprinted from the World, New York.

—— Amid Ancient Moqui Ruins. The Famous Snake Dance.

Times, Washington, September 23, 1894.

—— With the Snake Dancers.

Call, San Francisco, January 22, 1894.

—— Moqui Snake Dance.

Scimitar, Memphis, October 31, 1895.

—— The Moqui Snake Dance.

Sun, New York, October 4, 1894.

—— Hideous Rites.

Globe, Utica, October 18, 1895.

[1] From the varied and scattered newspapers and magazines in which accounts of the Snake dance have been published and read, it is almost impossible to make this bibliography complete. Reviews of works on the Snake dance, of which I have ever thing, are not mentioned.

The author has not completed his studies on the Snake dance, and would be glad to communicate with other students on this subject. The more important articles on the Walpi Snake dance of 1895 and 1896 are mentioned in the Journal of American Ethnology and Archaeology, Vol. IV.

318

INDEX

Page

AAPA, see APA.

ABANI day symbol discussed............... 22
ACATL day symbol discussed............... 243
—, meaning of........................... 227
Access to cliff villages.......... 104, 105, 158
ACOMA, snake dance at............... 203, 215
—, structural development of.............. 155
ACTIVITIES of mankind................... xvi
ADOBE the latest aboriginal............... 160
— construction in pueblo region........... 162
— walls in Casa Blanca........ 105, 106, 151
AGE of ruin determined by glaciering..... 151
— of trephined crania........... 18, 20, 72
AGUAL day symbol discussed.............. 249
AGRICULTURE of the Navaho.............. 67
AH day symbol discussed................. 245
AHAU and dowel symbols compared....... 225
— day symbol discussed.................. 252
AHPUUG-BALAM, a Maya deity.......... 344
AKBAL day symbol discussed............. 333
AK phonetic value of.................... 222
AKAB, definition of..................... 241
AKBAL symbol in Maya calendar......... 231
ALGONQUIAN languages, study of........ lxxiv
ALTAR, absence of, at Cipactori......... 277
—, time for erection of.................. 277
— see ANTELOPE ALTAR, SNAKE ALTAR.
ALVARADO-LEON, señor, services rendered
    by................................... lxiii
AMULET wearing in recovery............. 23
AMULET, absence of trephined skulls at.. 13
ANIMALS, domestic, trephined........... 13
AMULETS used in Tusayan ceremony...... 205
ANTELOPE ALTAR at Cipactori........... 278
— at Cañopari.......................... 287
— at Oraibi............................ 290
—, further description of................ 244
— of Tusayan discussed................. 296
—, time for preparation of........... 273, 264
ANTELOPE CHIEF, performances of.... 277, 244
ANTELOPE DANCE at Cipactori....... 277, 278
— at Oraibi............................. 290
ANTELOPE MESA at Oraibi etc....... 291, 297
ANTELOPE PRIESTS, number of.......... 245
— in Cañopari snake dance.............. 246
—, performances of, at Oraibi........... 246
—, why so called....................... 246
ANTHROPOLOGY, classification of........ xlvi,
                                    LXII, lix, lxi
—, development of...................... xvi
ANTIQUITY of trephining.......... 12, 20, 72
APACHE, study of the........... xxiii, xxvii
APE day symbol discussed............... 220
—, definition of........................ 228

Page

APPA, see APE.

APPROPRIATION of funds, change in...... 103
ARCHEOLOGY remains in Sonora.... xxxvi, lxviii
ARCHEOLOGY, work in......... xix, xx, xxvi,
                        xxiii, xxvii, xxx, xxxv, xxxvii,
                            xl, xlix, xlvii, l, lvi, lxvi-lxix
ARCHITECTURE of cliff ruins............ 133
—, pueblo, character of................. 133
—, pueblo, development of........... 91, 133
ARIZONA, cliff ruins of Cañyon de Chelly, 73, 106
— see CLIFF DWELLINGS.
ARMY OF THE WEST, conquest by........ 79
ARROW GAMES, study of................ lxxv
Attributes in Oraibi antelope dance...... 202
— in Oraibi snake dance................ 203
—, performance of the.................. 204
ASPERGILLS at Oraibi altar............. 202
— in Cipactori snake dance............. 204
— in Oraibi snake dance................ 204
ATL day symbol discussed............... 247
—, meaning of.......................... 222
ATLANTA EXPOSITION, Bureau exhibit at.. lxxix
ATTITUDE, cliff ruins attributed to...... 101

BAKAB, definition of................... 242
BAKLIN-CHAAM, a Maya deity........... 345
BALAM day symbol discussed............ 248
BALCHE, a ceremonial drink............. 273
BALCHE, definition of................... 242
BANDELIER, A. F., cliff ruins described by.. 91
BANDELIER, A. F., collections by, in Peru.. xxxi
— on classification of pueblo ruins....... 99
BANDOLIERS in Oraibi dance........ 202, 204
BASKETS at Tusayan altar............... 270
BAT, how regarded by Central Americans.. 225
— Indis in Cañyon de Chelly............ 137
BATAB day symbol discussed............ 241
BAXTER, S. M., account of snake dance by.. 271
BIGELOW, J. M., Cañyon de Chelly visited by.. 80
—, quoted on Cañyon de Chelly.......... 85
BEAN vines in Tusayan ceremony..... 205, 208
BEE, see BEER.
BEER, see BEER.
BELIEFS, primitive, defined............. 22
DAY symbol in Maya hieroglyphs.... 216, 245
Doors around cliff ruins... 121, 126, 127, 128, 137
— in cliff outlook..................... 131
BENEFICENCE shown in cliff ruins....... 131
BEYAL, meaning of..................... 243
BIBLIOGRAPHY of the Bureau........... cl-cxix
— of the snake dance................. 312
—, work in.............. xxi, xxiv, xxvii,
        xxviii, xxxvii, xxxix, xli, xliv, xlix, lxxvii

313

Page

BECKFORD, F. T., cliff ruins described by 61
BELLOWS, J. S., on statistics of trephining .. 19
Bird as a wind symbol 219
— symbols in the codices 219, 220, 222, 223, 224
BIRDSALL, W. R., cliff ruins described by .. 61, 102
BLACK DEITIES of Maya codices 246
BLACK, —, on statistics of trephining 16
BOAS, FRANZ, work of LIV
BORGIAN CODEX, discussion of symbols in .. 212, 218, 219, 222, 244
—, earth symbol in 234
—, fire symbols in 230
—, sky symbol in 230
BOTTOM LANDS, house villages on 94
BOURKE, J. G., snake-dance studies by 277
BOW, ceremonial use of 270, 302, 304
BOW LOOMS used in cliff-dwelling masonry .. 98, 100
BOTH in snake dance 302
BRASSEUR DE BOURBOURG, on symbol interpreted by 238
—, on definition of ak 245
—, on definition of chac 248
—, on definition of chacpoc 233
—, on definition of hok 241
—, on definition of kan 234
—, on definition of koz 238
—, on definition of ttac 243
—, on derivation of chuen 240
—, on Mexican mythology 221
—, on origin of cib token symbol 223
—, on the akab-cusan symbol 246
—, on the beaak symbol 246
—, on the germ symbol 244
—, on the monk day symbol 222
—, on the ttac symbol 244
BRETON, meaning of 232
BRINTON, D. G., bee symbol interpreted by .. 246
—, on dream symbol in Maya codex ... 224, 234
—, on meaning of certain symbols .. 218, 227, 230, 238
—, interpretation of light symbol by 237
—, interpretation of oc symbol by 230, 240
—, Maya and Zapotec names harmonized by .. 227
—, on definition of chien 238
—, on definition of chacan 245
—, on definition of ayo 242
—, on definition of camapan 240
—, on definition of akab 234
—, on definition of chinax 236-239
—, on definition of ch 244
—, on definition of reepal 238
—, on definition of yaxche 237
—, on definition of kic 242
—, on definition of koz 245
—, on definition of kanal 234
—, on definition of tarpal 235
—, on definition of tea 233
—, on definition of wakin 231, 232
—, on derivation of caban 245
—, on derivation of chicchan 230
—, on derivation of akava 243
—, on derivation of pops 235
—, on derivation of huul 236
—, on derivation of mani 234
—, on derivation of malax 238
—, on maggot sign in the codices 233
—, on the black deities 246

Page

BRINTON, D. G., on the cain day symbol 242
—, on the four-winds symbol 218
—, on the chacan symbol 239
—, on the Maya calendar 225
—, on the month name ttc 255
—, on origin of gubbe symbol 222
—, on origin of mecu symbol 221
—, on the rabbit in Indian mythology .. 223
—, on the term ni 219
—, Zapotec terms interpreted by 216
BROCA, PAUL, cited on primitive trephining .. 17, 18, 19
BROOM symbol in the codices 244
DELLENBAUGH, see WHEELER.
DELECARLIA, a Maya deity 244
BUNSEN-BEAKER in Troano codex 242
BURIAL-CISTS in Casa Blanca 138
— in cliff ruins discussed 136
— see CHIQUI NATANA.
BOTTERIES in Casa Blanca 118, 142
— in cliff ruins 118, 126, 128
— in kivas 177

Ca symbol of LANDA 242
CAB, definition of 235
— symbol, explanation of 235
CABAN symbol discussed 205, 230, 234
CABOK, definition of 247
CABRERA, —, on title of a Tzental manuscript 222
CACAO symbol in the codices 234, 238
CAONHEE, meaning of 245
CABOAN day symbol discussed 230
CALENDAR, Maori, day defined in 245
— of cenie ceremonies 176
— of the Maya .... xxv, xxvi
—, signification of 221
CAMAZOTZ in Central American mythology .. 239
CAMEY day symbol discussed 201
Can day symbol discussed 230
CABEL day symbol discussed 235
CASAVE, trephined crania from 13, 14
CARTALOUETS in Tusayan ceremony .. 280
CASTON DE COMLET, accessibility of .. 62
—, memoir on cliff ruins of 73-106
—, location of 64
— see CLIFF DWELLING.
CASTON DEL MUERTO, location of 64
—, ruins in, described 61
GLIOK day symbol discussed 230
CAPAL, definition of 242
CARDINAL POINTS, birds symbolic of the .. 218
—, corn symbolic of 201
—, observed in ceremonies 202, 277
—, snakes deposited at 301, 302
—, symbolized by colors 217, 247
—, symbols of, in the codices .. 224, 242, 227, 230
—, winds symbolic of 218
CARDONAL influence in Pueblo 1-11
CASA BLANCA, a name of two cliff dwellings .. 143
— described 104-211
— described by Simpson 70
— local construction in 102

Page

CANAL FRANCA, notched doorway in 184
CANAL GRANDES, investigation of, in Gila
   river remains 196
CASTAÑEDA, PEDRO DE, narrative of 11v
CAUAC day symbol discussed 239
CAVE RUINS, classification of 113
— village in Canyon de Chelly 97
CAVERN symbol in Mexican pictography ... 232
OCCELOTXAL, meaning of 254
Cib symbol in Dresden codex 240
— symbol discussed 241
CEREMONIAL CHAMBER, see KIVA.
CEREMONIES, scale, turned on 297–302
Ce', phonetic value of 210.230
CIFAL, meaning of 233
CHAATY day symbol discussed 256
CHAC, a Maya rain god 208.230
— deified 224.231
— symbol in Dresden codex 225–230
CHALCHIULT, meaning of 230
CHACMOOL, definition of 201
CHACO and old-world ruins compared 9
CHAMPOLLION, —, Egyptian negative signal
   by 232
CHAAN, meaning of 200.221
CHAPIN, F. H., cliff ruins visited by 61
— on openings in Mancos ruins 159
— on kiva decoration 153
CHARNAY, DESIRÉ, day symbol copied by ... 207
—, battlemented structures figured by 250
Che, definition of 230
CHEN, definition of 230
CHELLY, origin of name of 79
—, see CANYON DE CHELLY.
Chi, definition of 243
CHIC day symbol discussed 254
CHICCHAN day symbol discussed 238, 239, 243
CHIUH, phonetic value of 229
CHICABAN, meaning of 230
CHIUE, meaning of 230, 262
CHIMEH, meaning of 233
— symbol in Maya codex 225
CHISBA day symbol discussed 257
—, meaning of 232
CHICALPOPOCA comet, interpretation of
   mythic concept in 271
CHICKET-LIKE STRUCTURES discussed 145–246
— in Casa Blanca 119
— in cliff kivs 155, 159
— in cliff outlook 144
— in cliff ruins 119
— in Mummy Cave ruin 132, 135, 126
CHITAL day symbol discussed 229
CHICAB day symbol discussed 256
CHRONOLOGY of cliff-dwelling masonry ... 102, 105, 164,
    117, 120, 125, 127, 142, 144, 146, 150, 154, 158, 160
CHIN LEE VALLEY, ruins in 80
CHUHMALA, a Zapotec goddess 245
CHULLA, see CHELLA.
CHOAB symbol in Tonno codex 234
CHUEN, meaning of 237
CHUCO, meaning of 245
CHUCEB, meaning of 234
CHUECA, equivalent to xolotl 238
CHOOPE, meaning of 237
CHRISTIANITY, how regarded by the Hopi .. 299

CHUAC symbol in Maya hieroglyphs 224
CHVE, meaning of 232
CHI'EN, significance of 233
CHUTS and ethel symbols compared 227, 228
— day symbol discussed 232, 243
CHUECHE, definition of 243
CHUY, meaning of 233
CHUTO, meaning of 232
CI day symbol discussed 254
—, definition of 243
Cib day symbol discussed 234, 235
CIB symbol discussed 231
— symbol in Dresden codex 239
— symbol in Tonno codex 239
CIPACTLI symbol discussed 207, 242
— symbol in Borgia codex 213
CIPACTOUY snake ceremony described 277–298
— snake ceremony at 272, 276, 296
Cist, burial, excavation of 101
—, burial, in cliff ruins 64, 120
—, see BURIAL CIST; NAVAHO; MOGOLLON CIST.
CLARK, localization of, in pueblos 184
CLASSIFICATION of canyon ruins 93, 96
— of Peruvian brickbuilding 17, 91
— of pueblo ruins 96, 164
—, see ANTHROPOLOGY.
CLAVIGERO, F. S., on signification of Mexican
   term 244
CLIFF RUINS, classification of 96
— of Canyon de Chelly, memoir on ... xv-i, 73–160
—, researches among .. xix, xx, xxiii, xxvi, xxvii,
       xxx, xxxvii, xl, xlvi, xlvii, l, lxi, lxvii
CLIMATE of cliff ruin region 63
CLOTHING, see CEREMONY.
—, Loti's statements compared 250
— in the codices 275, 296
— in Tusayan sand picture 270, 297, 300
— on Oraibi kiva 300
— on Tusayan altars 181, 300
COCOPA, snake dance among the 311
CHAPATU day symbol discussed 250
COLLECTION of terpiained canals 90
— made by the Bureau .... xiii, xiv, l, liii, lviii
CODEX symbols in the codices 253, 256
— in Tusayan sand picture 273
— of Tusayan altar 275–279, 297, 301
COMANCHE, study of the .... xxiii, xxviii
COMB-LIKE CHARACTERS in Maya codex .. 224
— in Dresden codex 243
CONTRACTIVE expedients in cliff-dwelling .. 170
CANE, see CAUAC.
COMPOVA, —, on meaning of magoie 229
— on meaning of quil-lalen 201–230
Corn carried in Hopi dance 303
— ceremony in Tusayan 301
— destruction in Tonno codex 217
— in Hopi mythology 207
— cultivated by the Navaho 81
— vine compared with snake shoes 304
—, significance of 239
— symbols in the codices 216, 234, 242
— symbols of cardinal points 301
— used in Tusayan ceremony 278, 300, 301
—, see MEAL.
CORN ear in Maya hieroglyphs 216, 217, 230
CORN-MAID images on flute altar 300

Page

CORN-MAID personated in Hopi dances.... 300
CORNSTALKS in Cherokee antelope dance... 233
— in Hopi snake dance................ 284, 300
— in Oraibi kind....................... 287
CORNMEAL codex, color-symbol in...... 254
—, cross day symbol in................ 250
—, chaos symbol in.................... 241
—, cloud symbol in................... 221
—, discussion of symbols in........... 204, 241
—, ab symbol in....................... 242
—, te symbol in....................... 240
—, ben symbol in...................... 250
—, snake symbol in................... 237
—, re symbol in....................... 228
—, phonetic elements of symbols in.... 220
COMMERCE of the Hopi............... 202-204
— of the Mayas....................... 220
COSTUMES in Tusayan ceremony....... 221,
    234, 294, 295, 294
COTTONWOOD carried worn in snake dance. 300
— LEAVES in Tusayan ceremony .. 286, 290, 293, 294
— not used in Cheyenne snake dance... 284
CORTOPLAXTUS day symbol discussed..... 222
CRADLE, see TRUNDLING.
CRESSON, H. T., review of work of...... xxvi
Cross symbol in the codices............ 232, 239
CROW, meaning of...................... 247
CUCURBACH, meaning of............... 206, 261
CUETZPALLI day symbol discussed...... 224
—, meaning of......................... 227
CUITE, see EUTE.
CUMMY symbol in the codices........... 239
CUSOPAVI snake ceremony at........ 275, 297-300
CUTS pecked in rock................... 136
CREVILEZZA incisions in primitive trephin-
    ing................................. 25
CUSHING, F. H., on cardinal points in Zuni
    cosmogony......................... 167
—, on ceremonial fire................. 170
—, on ceremonial renewal of kivas... 177
—, on cliff ruins..................... 182
—, on marking of kiva hatchway...... 186
—, on primitive surgery.............. 11
—, on scarred skulls................. 45
—, researches by......... xxxiv, xxxvi, xxxvi,
    xxxvii, xxxix, xli, xliv, xlix, li, lvi, lxxv
CUTE, see EUTE.
CUTO, trephined crania from.......... 14, 15
CYPLODERMA of Indian tribes... li, lvi, lxiv, lxxii
—, see SERGOUNT.

DANCE, see SNAKE DANCE.
DAY deities in Maori calendar......... 205
— names in Maya and Mexican calendars.. 205
— SYMBOL in Tusayan codex.......... 221
— of the Maya year........ xxv, 204-241
DEATH GOD of the Mexicans.......... 215
— symbol as a day symbol............ 225
DECORATION of cliff-house walls....... 162,
    200, 213, 221, lii, 169, 177-201
DEER symbol in the codices.......... 223, 224
DEFENSE, absence of motive for, in cliff
    ruins............... 161, 142, 154, 156, 175, 180, 181
—, home villages located for........... 111

Page

DEFENSE, loopholes as evidence of........ 175
—, expedients for, in cliff dwellings..... 170
DEFENSIVE sites, to what attributed.... 91
DETTER, day in Maori calendar......... 205
DEGENERACY, classification of.......... xvi?
DEVELOPMENT of cliff dwellings........ 100
— of pueblo architecture............... 125
DILEMMAS by primitive inquirers....... 43
DINWIDDIE, WILLIAM, crania photographed
    by................................... 16
—, work of......... xx, xxii, xxiii, xxvi, xxvii,
    xxix, xxxiii, xliii, xlv, lxvii, lxii, lxvii
DISSECTION, facial, of Peruvian crania... 43
DISTRIBUTION of cliff ruins in its Chelly... 183-187
—, see CLASSIFICATION.
DIVINATION in scrapery................ 13
DOG-EAR symbol in the codices......... 236
DOG-EYE symbol in Mexican codices.... 242
DOG traders, sacrifice of.............. 241
DOG-LIKE ANIMALS in the codices.... 224, 225
DOG SYMBOL in Dresden codex......... 226
— in Maya codex..................... 226
DOLLS, Hopi, symbolism of........... 301
DORSEY, Abbé EN., references by, to Choc
    Blancs.............................. 30
DOORWAYS in cliff dwellings.......... 102,
    111, 121, 128, 254, 164, 313, 184
—, notched, in cliff dwellings......... 120, 184
— partially closed.................... 166
—, see OPENINGS.
DORSEY, J. O., obituary of........... lxxxii
—, work of......... xx, xxiv,
    xxvii, xxxi, xxxvi, xxxvii, lxci, lxxiii
DOTS connected with Maya glyphs...... 220,
    224, 225, 226, 241, 245, 254
DRAIN in Casa Blanca................ 119
DRESDEN codex, color symbol in....... 262
—, abal symbol in.................... 221
—, ben symbol in.................... 245
—, bird symbols in.................. 225, 241
—, birds-feathers symbolized in...... 247
—, cities day symbol in.............. 224
—, canes day symbol in.............. 230
—, ceh symbol in.................... 240
—, chos symbol in................... 223-226
—, chuen symbol in.................. 241
—, cib symbol in.................... 232
—, cimi symbol in................... 223
—, discussion of symbols in......... 213,
    214, 248, 256, 259, 263
—, ab symbol in.................... 243
—, ik symbol in.................... 244
—, ix symbol in.................... 243
—, ben symbol in................... 250
—, hog-nose deity in................ 245
—, men symbol in.................. 247
—, mol symbol in.................. 244, 268
—, muluc symbol in................ 227, 228
—, oc symbol in................... 229
—, Quetzal symbol in............. 234
—, serpent symbol in.............. 246
—, sol symbol in.................. 235
DRUM SYMBOL in Maya codex........ 234
DUCK personated in Hopi ceremony.... 301
DURBIN, C. S. J., lny figures modeled by.. lviii
DUTTON, C. R., cliffside region described by.. 92
DZACATAN, significance of........... 234

Page

E day symbol discussed 263
EAGLE, see FEATHERS.
— represented in the codices 231
EAR, see DISK-EAR.
EARTH symbol in Borgian codex 256
EARTH DEITY in Troano codex 246, 257
EARTHMOTHER symbol in Maya hieroglyphs ... 254
EARTHQUAKE symbol in the codices 256
Eb day symbol discussed 243
EDZNA day symbol discussed 246
ECCLESIASTICAL, — constitution of teotihing .. 35
Eginau day symbol discussed 246
Ek day symbol discussed 243
EKSTATL day symbol discussed 215, 229, 230
EKAN day symbol discussed 243
ELEVATION, method of, in trephining 66, 69
EL-MORRO, Navaho name of Canyon de
Chelly 85
ENCINAS, PASCUAL, services rendered by lxiii
ENVIRONMENT, villages sites influenced by ... 182
ERRON, A. DE, Arctic snake determined by 285
ETHNOLOGY defined .... xvi-xvii
ETZB day symbol discussed 243
EXCAVATION represented in Maya glyphs 255
EXPLANATION to the figures .... lxi-lxvii
EYE, day symbol in Maya codices 242
— in Maya glyphs 255
EZNAB, see EDZNAB.

FACIAL DECORATION in Tusayan ceremony 183
— of Cipiaktai snake priests 200
— in Oraibi snake dance 204
FARMING implements discussed 143
FARMING villages, cliff ruins classed as 120
— of the pueblos 159
FEASTING during Tusayan snake dance 206
FEATHER deposited on Tusayan altar 204
FEATHERED STRINGS in Cipiaktai ceremony ... 177
— on Cakwpsii altar 203
— on Oraibi altar 201, 203
FEATHERS, antelope priests decorated with 203
— in Oraibi ceremony 201, 204
— in snake-dance ceremony 206
— in Tusayan ceremony 171, 195
FEJERVARY CODEX, bird symbol in 230
—, reference to symbols in 230
FEATHERS, disease of, on Cipiaktai altar 177
— in Oraibi kiva 205
— on Oraibi antelope altar 204
FEWKES, J. W., research by, on Tusayan
snake ceremonies .... lxxxvii, xcvii, 267-312
—, on cardinal directions in ceremonies 197
—, researches by .... lix, lxix
FIELD DEITIES in Dresden codex 239
FINANCIAL STATEMENT of the Bureau xxiv
FIGURES used as captives 31
FIRE SYMBOL in the codices 210, 219, 234, 257
FIREPLACE, see CHIMNEY-LIKE STRUCTURE.
FOOT symbol in the codices 242, 243
FLETCHER, ROBERT, on primitive trephin-
ing 12, 16, 17, 26, 27
FLINT symbol in Borgian codex 256
FLOORS of cliff dwellings discussed 245, 252
FLORIDA, archeologic researches in lvi

GAMES, primitive, study of lxxv
GATSCHET, ALBERT S., researches by .... xxi,
    xxiv, xxxiii, xxxiv, xxxvi, xxxix,
    xli, xliv, xlix, lii, lviii, lxxiii, lxxv
GATE, see KAT.
GEOGRAPHY of cliff-ruin region 81
GEOLOGY of cliff-ruin region 82, 83
GODS MOTHER of the Hopi 240
GHANAN day symbol discussed 239
GILL, DELANCEY W., work of lxxix
GOODE, G. BROWN, acknowledgments to xiii
GOPA, definition of 256
GOPA day symbol discussed 243, 256
GOURD in Oraibi antelope dance 202
— placed on Oraibi altar 203
— used in Tusayan ceremony 200, 201, 203
GRANARY structures in cliff ruin 63
—, see CIST.
GRASS symbol in the codices 244
GREENING, see RAINING.
GUCU, meaning of 229
GUCUMATZ day symbol discussed 229
GUERDE, see GOURD.
GUECA day symbol discussed 229
GUELA-GUELA, definition of 229
GUI day symbol discussed 219
GUII day symbol discussed 229
GUILLOO day symbol discussed 229
GUPA, definition of 256
GUZMAN, —, on meaning of Xam 229

HAND symbol in the codices 257
HAIR, absence of snake ceremony of 273
HANUMAN, a Hindu monkey god 221
HARRISON, R. C., on ruins in Canyon de
Chelly 86
HAWAIIAN and Central American linguistic
similarities 256
— and Zapotec terms compared 256
— mythology, monsters in 214
HAX, meaning of 229
HAZARD, C. D., cliff-dweller collection of xxxi
HEAD symbol in Dresden codex 235
HENTY, meaning of 229
HEMP figures in Mexican codices 211
HEPASTOTHEUM defined 22

Page

HICHCAR, see XALINCAR.

HENDERSON, A., as authority for probabili.. 243
—, on Maya names of Venus.................. 249
—, on meaning of calveir 234
—, on meaning of cacaca 254
—, on meaning of ach and hix........... 249, 261
—, on meaning of chac................... 220
—, on meaning of chackeog................. 229
—, on meaning of chicken................. 230
—, on meaning of eb................... 245, 251
—, on meaning of chuuch................ 237
—, on meaning of chan................... 242
—, on meaning of ben................... 223
—, on meaning of imablle................ 241
—, on meaning of kanka................. 234
—, on meaning of manik................. 234
—, on meaning of 234
—, on meaning of mol................... 226
—, on meaning of pacca................ 217
—, on meaning of pol................... 208
—, on meaning of various Maya terms... 247
—, on meaning of cochah............. 239
—, on meaning of caba............... 221
—, on meaning of yaxsahil............. 217
—, on meaning of yakhol............ 213
—, on phonetic value of ah........... 218
—, on the akbal ox symbol........... 206
—, on the chuen symbol............. 214
—, on the term ahah............... 225
HERALDRY, Kiowa, study of........... lxv-lxvi
HERBS attached to prayer sticks........ 296
HEWITT, J. N. B., researches by...... xxvi, xxiv, xxvii, xxix, xxxvii, xxxix, xli, xliv, xliii, lii, lviii, lxviii, lxxii, lxxiv
HION, phonetic value of............... 230
HIEROGLYPHS, work in........ xix, xxii, xxvi, xxvii, xxix, xl, xli, xlviii, l, lv
HILLERS, J. K., crania photographed by... 23
HINDU MYTHOLOGY, monsters in........ 214
—, wind god in.................... 221
HIX, see BALAM; IX.
HOCAL, phonetic value of.............. 229
HODGE, F. W., list of Bureau publications by............. xi-xviii
—, on Kansas and Tusoan snake clans.. 304
—, on origin of Kansas snake dance.... 309
—, on origin of Sia snake dance...... 309
—, researches by........ xx, xxiii, xxvi, xxvii, xxviii, xxxvii, xl, xliv, xlvii, lil, lvi, lxxi, lxxvii
HOFFMAN, WALTER J., memoir by, cited.. liv
—, work of.................... liii
HOE definition of............... 241
HOKOL symbol discussed............. 219
HOLMES, W. H., cliff ruins described by... 93
—, on chimney-like structures........ 164
—, researches by........ xix, xxi, xxiv, lxxvi
HONEY symbol in Troano codex........ 258
HOOCE, meaning of............... 238
HOPI origin of certain cliff ruins...... 166
—, study of ancient ruins of the....... lxix
—, tradition regarding cliff ruins...... 191
—, see TUSAYAN.
HOPI PEOPLE of Tusayan............. 297
HUASTECA, hieroglyph cities from.. 13, 14, 15, 16
HUCK, meaning of.................. 234

Page

HUMMO symbol in the codices............. 229
HUUAMU day symbol discussed........... 341
HUPAPU, in Central American mythology.. 225
HURAKAN in the Popol Vuh........ 220, 221

IOM day symbol discussed........... 215
II, see QUII.
IK symbol in Maya calendar.......... 215
ILLUSTRATIONS, preparation of...... lxxix
IMAGES in Hopi ceremony........... 300
IMIX symbol discussed............. 207
INOM symbol discussed........... 207
INGA SANTA in PETROVICH CODEX..... 12, 20
INOAPHAWEX, disease treated by..... 69, 70
INSTRUMENTS used in primitive engraving... 11, 17, 27, 20, 22, 23, 24, 25, 26, 33, 35, 72
—, see STONE IMPLEMENTS.
IRRIGATION, prehistoric, in Sonora...... lxvii
ITLAN, possible derivation of........ 215
—, see KAELI-WALLI.
ITZAMNA, a Maya deity......... 243-241
—, elements of the term.......... 253
IRREVERSIBLE day symbol discussed.... 209
IX day symbol discussed.......... 243
IXCHEBELIAX, a Zapotec goddess..... 225
IXCHEL, a Maya deity........... 241

JACAL construction in Casa Blanca..... 100
—, construction in pueblo region..... 100
JACKSON, W. H., cliff ruins described by... 90, 91
JAVANESE, mythic birds of the....... 220
—, mythic monsters of the....... 226
JUGGLERY in savagery............ 12

KASTLE, torchlight practiced by the....... 16, 17, 18, 19, 40
KAK symbol in Maya hieroglyphs....... 229
KAT symbol discussed......... 214, 230, 242
KAVAN, see KAN.
KAKOLS, definition of........... 229
KANEL, meaning of............ 243
—, see CANEL.
KANHEL, definition of.......... 241
—, symbol in Maya codices....... 242
KAPAM, definition of.......... 262
K'AT day symbol discussed...... 229
KATELMET, researches among the...... lxv
K'ATIC, see K'AT.
KAWAIKA colony in Tusayan....... 208, 210
KAYAB symbol, use of........... 200
KEAM, T. V., burial cist excavated by.... 101
KELHLAN and Hopi snake dance compared.. 305, 300-311
— words in Hopi snake dance....... 306
KERN, R. H., Casa Blanca sketched by... 75
KI, definition of........... 243
KIVAS of antelope priests......... 232
— of Ushopavi snake priests........ 232
— of Oraibi snake dancers....... 234
— of Tusayan described....... 230-233

Page

Ker symbol in the codices............ 220, 235, 240
KINGSBOROUGH, Lord, skull glyph pictured
by 250
KINCHHAHIC represented in the codices.. 210, 218, 219
KIN-FA-S-EAL, Navaho name of Casa Blanca 194
KIOWA, researches among the............. xxiii, xxvii, xli, xlii, l, liii, lv, lxv, lxix
Kiva and cliff-dwelling analogues....... 184
— or brush shelter...................... 90
— erected in Shumopovi ceremony........ 94
— function of, in snake dance.......... 320
— how represented at Oraibari.......... 340
— of Tusayan described................. 90
KIVAS, absence of, in farming villages. 134
— distribution of, in cliff ruins..... 107
— function of.......................... 308
— how entered.......................... 110
— how planned.......................... 341
— in cliff ruins...... 100, 105, 113, 119, 121, 124, 125, 127, 139, 140, 145, 163, 171–178
— in Mummy Cave ruin................... 116
— in Palachi ruin...................... 90
— in Tse-ni-ki-ni canyon.............. 163
— of Casa Blanca described............ 187
— of unusual size..................... 95
— origin of........................... 91
— prevalence of, in pueblo ruins..... 90
— make ceremonies performed in........ 278
KNIFE, meaning of..................... 223
KNIVES, used among Indians............ 289
KYACTLAN, elements of the term........ 223
KUTH, definition of................... 221
— symbol in Troano codex............. 240, 261

LAA, see GET; QER.
XAALA, see OUI.
LANA-AVI-XIAL, definition of.......... 262
LASA, see LAVA.
LACOTA, snake rites of................ 320
LALAKONTI ceremony of Tusayan........ 302
LIMAY, and ak symbols compared....... 240
— day symbol discussed............... 126
LAMMAT day symbol discussed.......... 126
LAVA day symbol discussed............ 261
LAND sessions, see ROYCE, C. C.
LANDA, —, akan symbol given by....... 200
—, ben symbol given by............... 242
—, ca symbol given by............. 234, 238, 242
—, caban day symbol given by......... 264
—, cauac day symbol given by......... 269
—, chicchan symbol given by.......... 229
—, cib symbol given by............... 252
—, cimi symbol given by.............. 237
—, cited on Father Abas.............. 241
—, cited on Maya sacrifices.......... 212
—, cuca symbol given by.............. 244
—, e symbol of....................... 224
—, ik symbol given by................ 243
—, form of ethel symbol given by.... 221
—, kayabal given by.................. 218
—, it symbol given by................ 245
—, interpretation of symbols by..... 263
—, ix symbol given by................ 245

Page

LANDA, —, men symbol given by........ 228
—, ni symbol given by................ 221
—, ocael symbol given by............. 223
—, o symbol interpreted by........... 243
—, on symbol given by................ 221
—, pax symbol given by............... 230
—, tixber symbol given by............ 237
—, v symbol given by............. 208, 221
—, xo day symbol given by............ 220
Lat-day symbol discussed............. 262
Lava day symbol discussed............ 261
Law of metamorphism.................. 21
Law of the development of fable...... 21
Le, meaning of....................... 248
Lax, meaning of...................... 264
Lex, meaning of...................... 262
LANGARET, meaning of................. 248
LEAA, see OUI.
LIBRARY, growth of the.............. xx, xxiii, lxix
LANOTER, Mr Joseph, surgical operations
by................................... 99
LITTE symbol in the codices......... 227
—symbolized by the rabbit........... 238
Limestone present at Oraibi altar... 204
— in the codices...... 210, 226, 227, 240, 261
— in Tusayan sand picture........... 204, 247
LODE symbol in Maya codices......... 263
—, meaning of....................... 263
LINGUISTICS, work in................ xx, xxiv, xxviii, xxxii, xxxvii, xxxix, xli, xliv, xlix, liii, lx, lviii, lxxii–lxxxv
Lintels of cliff-ruin openings... 102, 104, 106, 164
Litanitat symbolism of the Moqui.... 226
LIZARD remains in Maya codices.. 210, 217, 221, 224
LO day symbol discussed............. 241
— signification of.............. 231, 234
—, see DWELLING, LOG.
Loopholes in cliff houses........... 103
LUMHOLTZ, Carl, collection by....... xxxi
—, Mexican linguistic material of... xxi, xxviii, xxxvii, xxxix, xliv, xlix, lviii

MA, meaning of...................... 224
MAC, symbol for..................... 212
MACAW symbol in Maya codex......... 226
McGEE, W J, researches by...... xxvi, xxix, xxx, xxxiii–xxxv, l, liii, liv, lv, lviii, lxviii, lxxviii
— and Muñiz, M. A., memoir by, on prehistoric trephining..... lxxxvii, lxxxix, 3, 72
Maguey symbol in the codices....... 232
MAN-GAS, definition of............. 217
MALALAMAL, definition of........... 262
MALAY and Maya languages compared.. xxi, xxv, xxvi, xxvii, xxxii, xxxvi
— and Zapotec terms compared....... 262
— mythology, monsters in........... 224
MALINALTEPEC symbol in Mexican pictography............................. 244
MALLERY, GARRICK, obituary of...... lxxx
—, on Indian sign for the knife.... 202
—, on meaning of certain hand symbols.. 212
—, on Mexican cloud symbols........ 225
—, on the sign for negation........ 212
—, researches by............... xix, xxii, xxxi

Page

MALINALCO day symbol discussed 243
MANKRACVI ceremony of Tusayan 303
MANCOS CANYON, cliff ruins in 61
MANDALRY, meaning of 264
MAYIK day symbol discussed 232, 243
—, phonetic element of 257
MANTEODERA, —, cited on primitive trephin-
ing 71
MASON, corn introduced among the 222
— day deities of the 266
— heart symbolism of the 256
— mythic monsters of the 224
Mayan symbols in the codices 246
MASON, O. T., acknowledgments to xiii
—, work by, on Indian cyclopedia lxx
MASON, —, cited on primitive trephining .. 12
MASONRY deteriorated by plastering 163
— of cliff houses ... 88, 98, 101, 102, 164, 225, 226, 237,
    248, 252, 153, 144, 148, 149, 150, 158, 237
—, rude, in cliff houses 203, 253
— see CHINKING; MORTAR; WALLS.
MAT symbol in the codices 246
MATTHEWS, WASHINGTON, on Navaho traditions regarding cliff ruins 194
MAYA and Malay languages compared ...... xxii,
    xxv, xxvi, xxviii, xxxii, xxxvii
— day names of the 246
— glyphs, study of .... xlii, xxx
— year, day symbols of the, month on .. xxv,
    xxx,xxx

— see HIEROGLYPHICS.

MAZATL day symbol discussed 239
MEAL, sacred, at Oraibi altar 292
— in Cipaalovi snake dance 295
— in Oraibi snake dance 293
— in Tusayan ceremony 291,293
— symbolized on masks 295
— trees of Tusayan described 297
— circle about kiva 294
— in Cakeporvi snake dance 292
— in Oraibi snake dance 295
— cross in Tusayan ceremony 279,279
— races in Tusayan ceremony 279–280, 262
— see Corn.

MEDICAL PRACTICE among savages lxxxiii
MEDICINE, ancient Peruvian knowledge of .. 11
— bowl, at Oraibi altar 291,292
— at Tusayan altar 279
— carried in Oraibi snake dance ... 294
— in Cipaalovi snake dance 294
— in Oraibi antelope dance 297
— in Tusayan ceremony 292

MELON, see CANTALOUPE; WATERMELON.
MEN day symbol discussed 250
MENDOZA CODEX, corn symbol in ... 237
—, sun symbol in the 244
MERCURY, researches among the 81
MESA VERDE, cliff ruins of 61
METAL not used in primitive trephining. 60, 66, 65
MEXTLI TLI, day symbol of the 106
MICCAILHUITL, snake ceremony at ... 279
MINDELEFF, COSMOS, memoir by, on cliff
    ruins of Canyon de Chelly. xxxvii, xxi, 73–198
— on snake dance at Micchinovi ... 279
—, researches by .... xix, xx,
    xxii, xxiii, xxvi, xxxiv, xxxv, xxxvi,
    xxxviii, xl, xliii, xlvii, lxi, lxvii

MIGUELITO day symbol discussed 243
MOCCASINS of the Oti snake dancers .. 294
MONOGRAM, a Hopi summer village ... 92, 154
MON, symbol in Dresden codex 224, 250
MILLO day symbol discussed 227
MONKEY in Quiche mythology 329
— in Mexican mythology 324
— god of the Hindu 321
MONSTERS in Oraibi mythology 214
MONTEZUMA CANYON, location of 65
MOON symbol in Borgian codex 222
MOONEY, JAMES, researches by ...... xx,
    xxii, xxiii, xxv, xxvii, xxix,
    xxxvii, xli, xliv, liii, liv, lxvi, lxxi, lxxi
MORAN, THOMAS, Canyon de Chelly ruins
    visited by 82
MORTALITY of trephined subjects 66
MORTAR, character of, in cliff houses ...237, 248, 252
—, source of, in cliff-house building .. 164
—, see MASONRY; PLASTERING.
MOTIVE for primitive trephining 69
MOX, see IMOX.
MOXO day symbol discussed 243
MUAN, see IMIX.
MIXL, definition of 266
MOL, definition of 266
MOLK, see MEAL.
MULUC symbol discussed 266
— symbol in Dresden codex 258
MUMMIFICATION practiced by ancient Pe-
    ruvians 13, 44, 49
MUMMY CAVE RUIN, benches and buttresses
    in 177
— described 91, 113
—, kiva in 174
MUÑIZ, M. A., and McGEE, W J, memoir
    by, on primitive trephining ...... lxxxviii,
        lxxxviii, 3–72
MUÑIZ, —, cited on primitive trephining ... 12
MOYAL, definition of 266
MUYUCAL, etymology of the 250
MYTHOLOGY, work in ... xx, xxiv, xxviii, xxxi,
    xxxvii, xxxix, xli, xliv, lii, lvi, lxvi–lxxvi

NAA day symbol discussed 239
NAHUAN, meaning of 223
NAOLIN, meaning of 244
NAOYTCH, meaning of 221
NAHUATL, day names of the 246
—, see AZTEC.
NAHUI OLLI day symbol discussed ... 251
NAKWAKWOCI, see FEATHERED STRINGS.
NAVAHO, agriculture of the 41
—, attendance of, at snake dance ... 297
—, building material from cliff dwellings
    used by 164
— burials in cliff villages 168, 216, 213, 137, 138,
        129, 134, 139, 142, 144, 159, 153, 158, 167–170, 197
— burials, see CAVES.
— cliff ruins utilized by 46, 164, 167
—, expedition against the 70
—, granaries in cliff ruins 97
— houses sites in Canyon de Chelly .. 97
— houses, sites of 150

Page

NAVAJO, pueblos ruined by the 66
— occurrence in cliff dwellings 149
—, study of the .... xlvii–xlviii
— tradition of cliff dwellings 131,135
— trails in Canyon de Chelly 127
— walls in cliff outlooks 123
NECKLACES of shell discern 203, 204
—, see SHELL; TURQUOIS.
NECROLOGY of the Sarem .... hxxx
NECROMANCY in savagery 21
NELSON, —, cited on primitive trephining. 20
NEW MEXICO, see CLIFF DWELLINGS.
NEW YEAR, Mexican festival of the 244
NEW ZEALAND and Central American Re-
    public similarities 236
— and Zapotecans compared 282
—, see MAORI.
NU, signification of, in Maya 220
—, see UOL.
NICHES in kiva walls 172
NICHOLS, HENRY, cited on Maori ancestors. 224
NINE LORDS OF THE NIGHT in Borgian codex 229
NILA day symbol discussed 267
NON day symbol discussed 254
NORDENSKIÖLD, G., cliff ruins classified by. 90
—, cliff ruins described by 94
—, on a rear oval kiva 177
—, on chimney-like structures 168,169
—, on kiva decoration 188
—, on Mesa Verde masonry 160
—, on openings in Mancos ruins 162
NUTES DE LA VEGA, Bishop, on Central
    American deity 222
—, on the abbess symbol 236
NUTRIA, a Zuñi summer village 93,130

OBLATION practiced in savagery 23
—, see PURIFICATION.
OC day symbol discussed 239, 246
OCELOTL day symbol discussed 248
OON, meaning of 241
OCQUE, meaning of 241
OHUWA cloud symbol 229
OJO CALIENTE, a Zuñi summer village ... 93, 130
—, masonry of 159
OKCAMP, see TOCOAME.
OLLIN day symbol discussed 274
—, meaning of 265
OLMOS, Pedro de, Mexican interpreter writ-
    ings of xxxix
OLON symbol discussed 278
OPENINGS, absence of, in cliff houses ... 122
— in Casa Blanca walls 100
— in cliff kivas 125, 129, 175
— in cliff dwelling walls 122–124, 162, 177
— in Mummy Cave ruin walls 114
UQUIL, meaning of 241
ORAIBI, snake ceremony at ... 272, 286–290, 296
O'SULLIVAN, T. H., Casa Blanca photo-
    graphed by 99
OTOOH, meaning of 247
OUTLOOKS on restricted areas 160
— or farming niches discussed 173
OVEN-LIKE STRUCTURES in cliff ruins ... 177

Page

OTHER not an aboriginal feature 172
OXLAHUN day symbol discussed 261

PA-IA, definition of 240
PACHACAMAC, tryglyndd columns from ... 14, 15
PACHAH, definition of 247
PAHIC, meaning of 247
PAHO, see PRAYER-STICK.
PAINTING of bodies in Oraibi dance ... 286, 292, 296
— see FACIAL DECORATION; MASK PAINTING.
PAK, meaning of 247, 248
PAKAMACKEN ruin in Del Muerto 94
PAL, signification of 239
PALENQUE TABLET, cross symbol on 220
—, chore symbol on 241
—, day symbol on 237
—, ik symbol on 235
—, kex symbol on 250
—, kowal symbol on 265
PANTHER-LIKE animals in Dresden codex... 230
PAPAGO, collections from the 215, 216
—, ornaments among the .... xxxv,
                                xxxii, xxxiii, lxii
—, villages of the xxxv
PARAPHERNALIA of Oraibi snake dance. 289
— see CEREMONY.
PATANT symbol in Dresden codex 230
PASSAGEWAY in Casa Blanca 100
— in cliff dwelling 100
PAX symbol referred to 248
PEACHES, groves of, in Canyon de Chelly... 84
— introduced by Spaniards 84
PETAL, definition of 247
PETAH symbol in Maya codex 239
PET symbol in Maya codex 239
PETROGLYPH, application of term 240
PFLA-PALLARS, meaning of 241
PHASES, A., on Mexican cavern symbol... 250
—, on symbolism of worlds 244
PERESIANUS CODEX, caven day symbol in... 230
—, chore symbol in 241
—, ak symbol in 242
—, Caup symbol in 243
—, kan symbol in 250
—, vo symbol in 238
PENET, Pio, on meaning of chucheley...... 236
—, on meaning of chicchan 232
—, on meaning of cizin 234
—, on meaning of cimeh 237
—, on meaning of cib 232
—, on meaning of chuen 239
—, on meaning of kabau 235
—, on meaning of kab 240
—, on meaning of thel 238
—, on meaning of hombat 235
—, on meaning of imix 234
—, on meaning of ik 235
—, on meaning of ix 250
—, on meaning of muluk, chwoh 235
—, on meaning of quchicbal 237
—, on meaning of lak 248
—, on meaning of ben 241
PERU, primitive trephining in 5–73
PESCADO, a Zuñi summer village 93, 130
PETROGLYPHS in cliff villages 138

Page

PETROGLYPHS, see HIEROGLYPHS; PICTOGRAPHS.

PHILOLOGY defined .... xvii–xviii

—, see LINGUISTICS.

PHONETIC value of Maya hieroglyphs 209,
218, 222, 224, 228, 227, 238, 239, 241, 242,
247, 249, 253, 254, 255, 257, 259, 261, 263

PHONETICS, application of term 254

PICTOGRAPHS, preparation of lxxix

PICTOGRAPHY defined 22

PICTOGRAPHS in cliff ruins 66,
100, 112, 113, 126, 143, 144, 152, 179–181

— of Indians discussed xcv

—, see HIEROGLYPHICS.

PIBA day symbol discussed 223

PILLING, JAMES C., retirement of xlix

—, bibliographic work of .... xxxi,
xxxii, xxxv, xxxvii, xxxviii,
xxxix, xli, xlv, xlix, lxxvii

PARKER, V., Tzental patriarchate given by .. 202

PIPIL, day symbol of the 252

PEX, BARTOLOME DE, on meaning of certain symbol 246

PIZARRO, FRANCISCO, condition of mountains of 23

PLASTERING, effect of, on floor work 361

— of cliff ruin walls 112,
200, 221, 229, 240, 144, 149, 151, 160

— of kiva walls 221, 275

PLATES, trephined aperture covered by 66

PLATFORMS of masonry connected with cliff
ruins 173

PORCUPINE, dentition of 247

PORTER, J. H., account of Oraibi snake
dance by 273

POZOL VUH, bat bone mentioned in 122

—, mythic bird mentioned in 230

—, reference to monkey in 223

POPULATION of Casa Blanca 149

— of cliff dwellings 94, 175, 196

— of Pahahti-kini ruin 90

POST-MORTEM trephining, absence of ... 69, 72

PORTRAIT fragments in Casa Blanca 131

POWER, —, certain symbols interpreted by .. 234

POWELL, J. W., classification of primitive
beliefs by 23

—, Oraibi ceremony described by 260

PRAYER-STICKS at Tusayan altars 270

— in cosmoschily deposited 261

—, consecration of 268

—, delivery of, to snake chief 277

—, description of, in Tusayan ceremony ... 260

—, making of, in Tusayan ceremony 260, 281

— of Oraibi and Cipaulovi 264

—, prescribed length of 260, 264

—, presentation of, to racer 264

—, use of 260

—, used in Cipaulovi snake dance 265

— used in snake dance 260, 267

— used in Tusayan ceremony 263

PSALTER of the Maya 226

PRIMITIVE man mentioned in Peru, remains of .. 2–72

PRIEST/RIKERS, —, chief on primitive trephining 77

PROLIFERATIONS of the Fauces, list of lxxx

—, progress of .... xxv, xxvi, xxix,
xxxiii, xxxvii, xl, xliv, liv, lx, lxxxii

Page

PUCHAM, definition of 247

PUEBLO RUINS classified 90

—, see CLIFF DWELLINGS.

PURIFICATION ceremony in Tusayan 294, 295

— symbol in Troano codex 294

PUTNAM, F. W., cliff ruins described by ... 90

QI, definition of, ... 262

Q-TOK, meaning of, ... 221

QUAKCHIL day symbol discussed 216

QUEH day symbol discussed 222

QUETZAL symbol in Dresden codex 234

QUILL, see XIPIL.

QUIAHUITL day symbol discussed 216

QUICHÉ CAKCHIQUEL, day names of the ... 200

QUICHÉ myth, reference to monkey in 143

QUII day symbol discussed 216

QUIXAXA, meaning of 221

RABBIT in Indian mythology 216

— symbol in the codices 216

RACE, see SNAKE RACE.

RAIN, see CLOUD.

RAIN deity in Dresden codex 216

— in Troano codex 217

— of the Quiche 218

— of the Mexicans 215

RAIN symbol in Dresden codex 216

— in Troano codex 222

RAMIREZ, —, on Mexican wind and rain gods .. 216

RAMPOO employed in trephining 51, 55

RATTLES in Oraibi antelope dance 262

— used in snake dance 260, 264

— in Tusayan ceremony 261, 262

— of antelope booth 264

RECTILINEAR recesses in primitive trephining 56

RED RACE pottery, researches in ... . lx, lxix

RICHARDSON structures connected with cliff
village 126

REPARTADLA, definition of 262

RHOMBS, definition of 269

ROUNDELS of human bone, absence of ... 47

ROOF construction of Casa Blanca 109, 121

ROOFS of cliff dwellings discussed ... 163, 167

ROOMS, character of, in cliff dwellings ... 90, 162

RISBY, L. M., on the kamai symbol 240

ROYCE, C. C., preparation of monograph by ... xliii,
lv, lxxii

RUINS, pueblo, classified 90

—, see CLIFF DWELLINGS; PUEBLO.

SACRED MEAL in Tusayan ceremony 277

SALAMANDER, kamai, in Hopi legend 207

— of dog images 211

SANDAL and Central American similarities .. 204

— and Zapotec laws compared 242

SAND ceremonially sprinkled in field .. 260, 265

SAND picture at Cakaparel 227

— at Oraibi altar 261

— in Cipaulovi ceremony 271

Page

Inscriptions in Canyon de Chelly............ 94
SCALPING, origin of...................... 54
SCALPS worn as trophies................... 21
SCHELLHAS, P., on corn symbol in Maya
  hieroglyphs........................... 257
—, on death god symbol in codices......... 243
—, on origin of certain Maya symbol....... 245
—, on the black deities.................... 246
—, on the bat symbol................. 207, 208
—, on wind symbol in the codices.......... 250

SCOTT, N. M., collections by, in Peru...... xxxi
SERAPION, see KANTSOL.
SELER, EDWARD, algae symbol figured by.... 262
—, discussion of symbols by.............. 248
—, interpretation of certain symbols by....
  .... 216, 223, 232, 257
—, Dresden codex glyphs interpreted by... 256, 261
—, interpretation of bee symbol by........ 239
—, interpretation of maize symbol by...... 238
—, interpretation of oc symbol by.... 259, 260, 261
—, interpretation of Troano figures by.... 217
—, Maya and Zapotec names harmonized
  by..................................... 257
—, misinterpretation of symbols by........ 262
—, on certain bird-like figures........... 219
—, on certain deity symbols.............. 219
—, on corn symbol on Maya codices....... 257
—, on derivation of chuen............... 260
—, on derivation of pop.................. 259
—, on derivation of imix................. 262
—, on derivation of manik............... 261
—, on derivation of muluc............... 258
—, on derivation of oc.................. 255
—, on dot circle in Maya hieroglyphs..... 253
—, on meaning of ahau................... 263
—, on meaning of akbal................. 262
—, on meaning of cimi................... 263
—, on meaning of certain calendar names..
  .... 244, 245
—, on meaning of chifa................... 212
—, on meaning of ahau................... 263
—, on meaning of eb.................... 256
—, on meaning of akba.................. 253
—, on meaning of kayab................. 256
—, on meaning of kan................... 256
—, on meaning of the symbol............. 253
—, on meaning of naten, tetan........ 211, 222
—, on origin of bee symbol.............. 245
—, on origin of certain Maya symbol...... 245
—, on corn symbols in Borgian codex..... 272
—, on the black deities................. 246
—, on the muwan symbol................ 255
—, on the cauac symbol................. 210
—, on the chac symbol............. 209, 257, 258
—, on the ahau symbol.................. 243
—, on the eagle glyph.................. 231
—, on the cib day symbol............... 245
—, on the god-fire symbol.............. 243
—, on the imix symbol............. 257, 258, 260
—, on the ix glyph.................... 259
—, on the ben-ik-ix symbol............ 211
—, on the lamat symbol................ 226
—, on Maya calendar................... 245
—, on the iwa symbol.................. 254
—, on serpent symbol in Dresden codex... 250
—, on wind symbol in the codices........ 250

Page

SELER, EDWARD, on Zapotec interpretation
  of certain terms....................... 257
—, phoneticism of hieroglyphs not accepted
  by..................................... xlv, 213
SACRIFICE, researches among the.......... lii, lvi
Soul and Vamos relationship............. xlii
  , collections from the............ 204, 191
—, researches among the.............. xxxiii, lvii
SERPENT figures in the codices....... 250, 256
  — in Mexican pictography.............. 251
  — in Tzental pictography.............. 252
  — see SNAKES.
Serpent symbol in Dresden codex.......... 257
SET of trephined subjects............... 62
SHAWNEE LANGUAGE, study of..........
  .... xxi, xvi, xxvii, xxxii, xxix, xlv, lxxiv
Sheep introduced by Spaniards.......... 189
Shells sounds in Florida............... lviii
  — evidence in Tusayan ceremony....... 242
  — plate over trephined aperture....... 34
SHRINE in Chaculovi ceremony.......... 241
Sia and Hopi snake dance compared...... 316
  — kind of the........................ 307
  — snake dance of the............ 310, 316
SICA LANGUAGE, work in.............. lix,
  .... xxiii, xxvi, xxxvii
SIMPSON, J. H., Casa Blanca visited by.... 194
  — on Navaho expedition.............. 79
SINEWS improvised for Tusayan ceremony. 243
  — sacred meal symbolized on.......... 359
SITE of Tusayan ceremony at........... 370
SKIN, inaccessible, of cliff houses...... 61,
  .... 111, 121, 124, 163, 166
  — of pueblos, how determined........ 91
SKULL symbol in the codices....... 232, 235, 236
  — see CRANIAL TREPHINING.
SLING used by ancient Peruvians......... 11
SMOKING, ceremonial, by the Hopi....... 277,
  .... 241, 246, 266
SNAKES, how handled in Tusayan dance... 284
  — see SERPENT.
  — ceremonies, account of....... xxviii-xxix, 267-313
  — chief, performance of............. 277
  — dance at Cipaulovi............... 294-296
  — dance at Cuñopavi................ 295
  — dance at Oraibi.............. 298-300
  — dance, function of the............ 307
  — figures on Oraibi kilts........... 294
  — hunt at Tusayan................. 277
  — rattle and corn rattle compared.... 301
  — rattle discussed................. 302
  — people, union of, with their people.. 241
  — race at Cipaulovi............. 297-301
  — race at Oraibi.................. 298
  — symbol in Troano codex........... 247
  — whips described.................. 307
  — whips in Tusayan ceremony... 276, 279, 280, 284
SOCIOLOGY defined................... xvii
  — work in................... lx, lxxvii
SOUTHEAST in Tusayan ceremony..... 240, 302
SPECIALIZATION defined.............. xviii
Spasmodic trephining defined.......... 18
SOUTH SEA ISLANDERS, trephining among.. 17,
  .... 18, 69, 70
SPANISH intrusion in old dwellings, summary. 187
  — remains in Canyon de Chelly....... 193

Page

SHADES, sheep introduced by....   102
SPIDER WOMAN in Hopi mythology....   301
SQUIRRL in Cipactoni snake dance....   302
SUCHER, E. G., from skull collected by....   6, 12, 77
STAR SYMBOL in Maya codices....   222, 229
STEATITE QUARRY, study of....   xxiii, lxvii
STEPHEN, A. M., on Hopi tradition of cliff ruins....   151
STEVE, absence of, in cliff villages....   127
— see FOOT-SOLES.
STEVENS, J. L. bel-llesomnted structures figured by....   248
STEVENSON, JAMES, Canyon de Chelly visited by....   51
STEVENSON, M. C., on Keresan snake dance....   305, 308, 314
— on the Sia list....   307
— research by....   xx, xxiv, xxviii, xxxii, xxxvi, xxxix, xl, xliv, xlviii, lii, lvi, lxxv
STOLL, OTTO, on dedalities of sites....   302
— on signification of verb....   293
STONE IMPLEMENTS, absence of, in Cipactoni ceremony....   320
— absence of, at Oraibi altar....   297
— on Oraibi altar....   301
— used in trephining....   39
— see IMPLEMENTS.
STORAGE cists in cliff ruins discussed....   106, 117
— rooms in cliff village....   126, 132
— see CIST, GRANARY.
STORM GOD in Hindu mythology....   321
STRIX ANO in the cliff-ruin region....   24
SUMMER VILLAGES of pueblos....   82, 156
SUN SYMBOL in Hopi drama....   300
— symbol in the codices....   222, 226, 228
— worship in Tusayan....   307
SUNSET, primitive, method of....   77
— see TREPHINING.
SUTURES, condition of, in Peruvian crania....   23, 29, 30, 32, 34, 35, 36, 37, 42, 52, 62, 52
SYMBOLISM of the Kiowa....   lxvi
— value, in pueblo pictography....   124
— see DAY SYMBOLS.
SYDOSTYLE, work in....   xli, xlix, xlvii, xlvii, lxxvi, lxxvii, xli, xliv, xliii E
— see CYCLOPEDIA.

TABOO in sorcery....   31
— of children timber by Navaho....   152
TAMAYAN and Central American linguistic similarities....   329
TANIWHA, a mythic monster....   214
TAOS, a storycried pueblo....   152
— circular kivas at....   175
TARAHUMARI linguistic material....   xxxvii, xxxix, xli
TARMA, trephined cranium from....   13, 14, 15
TAX symbol, phonetic value of....   222
TAYLOR, RICHARD, cited on Maori lizard god....   214
— on Maori lizard symbolism....   204
TEPENAGOTY defined....   xvii
TECOMATL, day symbol discussed....   227
— definition of....   202
TECPATL, day symbol discussed....   228

Page

TECPATL, meaning of....   228
TECPILA, MALINATT, day symbol discussed....   234
TELLAO, definition of....   240
TEOTL, worn as trophies....   21
TELLA, day symbol discussed....   228
TEOTLALVEL, see TEOTL-ITONAL.
TEOTL-ITONAL, day symbol discussed....   231
TEOTOLOTL, signification of....   201
TEOTEOLOTL, signification of....   201
TEOTEOMATURGO motive in trephining....   24, 68, 70, 71, 72
THERAPEUTIC motive in trephining....   19, 68, 72
THOMAS, CYRUS, on day symbols of the Maya year....   lxxviii-xciv, 189-246
— researches by....   xlix, xxii, xxvi, xxx, xxxv, xxxviii, xl, xlii, xlvii, l, lv, lxxx
TICHORA god of the Quiche....   276
— symbol in Mexican hieroglyphs....   219
THOTON MONTH, see SIZE.
TIHU, meaning of....   293
DEGRADATIONAL in Mexican hieroglyphs....   242
TIHU symbol in the codices....   228
TITLE day symbol discussed....   228
— definition of....   200
TIKAL INSCRIPTION, ahau glyph in....   243
— the symbol in....   229
— lunar symbol in....   235
TIMBER, source of, for the Hopi....   106
— used in cliff-dwelling construction....   111, 112, 116, 121, 122, 124, 145, 171, 187
TIPON, absence of, in Cipactoni ceremony....   292, 302
— absence of, in Oraibi snake society....   300, 301, 304
— at Oraibi altar....   301
— of Oraibi antelope priests....   293, 302
— on Tusayan antelope altar....   299
— position of, on Cipactoni altar....   298
— used in Cipactoni ceremony....   293, 294
TITO in Hopi mythology....   301
TLALOC, a Mexican god....   324
— symbol in Borgian codex....   219
— symbol in Troano codex....   216, 227
TOCHTLI, day symbol discussed....   226
TOM day symbol discussed....   227
— meaning of....   226
TOMIL, a Quiche deity....   276
TOM, meaning of....   228
TOMA and Central American linguistic similarities....   329
— and Zapotec form compared....   269
TOO-QUIEN-PILLAPA, meaning of....   220
TRATTU among Indians....   24
— represented in Troano codex....   219
TOTEMS in sorcery....   31
TOTONTA ceremonies at Cipactoni....   279
TOTTO in Hopi mythology....   301
TOX day symbol discussed....   221
TOX COAMI, meaning of....   221
TRADITIONS regarding cliff dwellings....   126-151
TRANS in Congres de Utcally....   157
TREPHATIO injuries of Peruvian crania....   45
TRESSALL, HOWARD, died on mythic water monster....   214
TREPHINING in Peru, treated of....   lxxxix, x-79
TREPHINING found in Peru....   lxix, lxviii
TROANO CODEX, bird symbols in the....   221
— burden bearers symbolized in....   247
— ashen symbol in....   254

Page

TROANO CODEX, cases day symbol in...... 356
—, division symbol in................ 329
—, dance symbol in................... 341
—, sisal symbol in................... 322
—, earth god in...................... 319
—, corn symbol in.................... 327
—, discussion of glyphs in........... 314, 324, 326, 334, 336, 356, 361, 362
—, ek symbol in...................... 343
—, offrand day symbol in............. 356
—, ix symbol in...................... 348
—, oc symbol in...................... 339
—, caui symbol in.................... 343
—, yax symbol in.................... 347
—, snake symbol in.................. 347
—, symbolic figure in............... 318
TSE-GI, Navaho name of Canyon de Chelly. 29, 66
TSE-I-YA-KIN, Navaho name of Mummy Cave ruin........................ 112
TSE-OU-TSO-SI CANYON, location of...... 66
—, ruin in.......................... 104
TUSAYAN LANGUAGE, study of.......... xxi, xiii, xiv, xxix, lxiii, lxxiv
TUNICHA MOUNTAINS, reference to....... 34, 66
TURKEY SYMBOL in the codices....... 346, 361
TURQUOIS necklaces in Tusayan ceremony.. 282
TURTLE SHELLS in Tusayan ceremony..... 282
TUSAYAN, masonry of................. 162
—, migration to, of Towas.......... 168
—, snake ceremonies, memoir on...... xxvii-xxix, 267-312
—, villages of...................... xcviii
—, villages, location of, when discovered.. 25
—, see HOPI.
TYLOR, E. B., cited on religious concepts... 329
TU, phonetic value of.............. 718, 725
TZAC, definition of................. 341
TZEC, symbol in Dresden codex...... 342
TZENTAL, day names of the.......... 336
TU day symbol discussed........... 336
TZELTAL, definition of.............. 342
TZEQUIN day symbol discussed...... 356
TREE symbol in Maya hieroglyphs..... 336

UAR, signification of............... 329
URUGUAY, graved crania from...... 71, 85
UITZILOPOCHTLI god in Troano codex... 343
— in Troano codex................. 319
UOTAN, see VOTAN.

VEGETATION of cliff-ruin region...... 60
VRAMBOLA PETROGLYPH defined........ 18
VIENNESE CODEX, eagle symbol in.... 361
VOTAN day symbol discussed....... 321
—, significance of................. 321
VOTH, H. R., Oraibi rites studied by... 284, 286
VUCUB, signification of............. 329

WALLS, finish of, in cliff ruins.... 167, 313, 314, 315
—, retaining, in Canyon de Chelly..... 172
WALPI and Oraibi snake dance compared... 286
—, character of snake ceremony at.... 314
—, former location of............... 30
WALTHER, HENRY, work of.......... xxiii

Page

WAR-GOD fetish in Oraibi kiva........ 296
WARRINGTON, Col., Navaho expedition under.. 79
WATCH TOWERS and cliff dwellings analogous....................... 72
— of pueblos....................... 62
WATER-GARDENS in Cipaulovi catclysmic dance.......................... 283
— supply of Canyon de Chelly..... 93, 94
— symbolism in Tusayan.......... 341
— used in Tusayan ceremony...... 281
— vessels of Cipaulovi kiva....... 279
—, see APPENDIX; CHALCHI; RAIN.
WATERMELONS, vines of, carried in snake dance.......................... 306
— used in Cipaulovi snake race..... 304
— used in Tusayan ceremony...... 280
WEAPONS of ancient Peruvians....... 11
WHEELER SURVEY, archaeological work under............................ 66
WHORL, symbol in Troano codex....... 362
WHIP, see SNAKE WHIP.
WHITE HOUSE, see CASA BLANCA.
WHITEWASH used in Casa Blanca....... 160
— used in Mummy Cave ruin....... 125
— used on cliff houses........... 148
WHIZZER, absence of, in certain snake dances............ 303, 304, 305, 310, 311
— in Cipaulovi snake ceremony..... 304
WIND, effect of, on snake crop...... 317
— god in Hindu mythology........ 321
— gods of the Mexicans.......... 319
— in Mexican mythology.......... 321
— symbol in the codices.......... 322
— symbol in Mexican hieroglyphs.. 316, 317, 319, 320, 321, 322
— symbol, the bird as x.......... 319
WINDOW opening in cliff outlook..... 148
—, see OPENING.
WINSHIP, G. P., memoir by, cited..... 26
WITCHCRAFT practiced in savagery.... 21
WOMEN participants in snake dance... 306
WOOD, GEORGE M., work of......... lxxvii
WOOD symbol in the codices........ 362
WOODHOOD, ceremonial, among Indians.. 68
WORKING, trephining the result of.... 67
WYMAN, —, cited on primitive trephining.. 17

XACUTAR, definition of............. 344
XAR, meaning of................... 334
XIUHEUE, —, on definition of ek..... 344
— on meaning of certain Maya terms. 337
— on meaning of Imox............. 333
— on meaning of kan............. 336
— on meaning of oc.............. 339
— on meaning of pix............. 343
XIPE, a Mexican death god......... 343
XOCHITL day symbol discussed..... 356
XOME, meaning of................. 333
XOO day symbol discussed......... 334
XULUN, meaning of................ 335
XULMU, meaning of............... 335
XUPACAM, meaning of............ 335
XUL'S, meaning of............... 335
XUPACO, meaning of............. 336

	Page
Yaomi, meaning of	224
Yaqui and Papago compared	xxiv
Yarrow, H. C., on hives at Taos	175
Yax and ak symbols compared	249
— symbol of the Maya	241
Yaxha, form of, discussed	243
— symbol of the Maya	241
Year, Maya, day symbols of the	207, 208-209
Yellow, how represented in codices	228
Yib, signification of	254
Yik, see Balam.	
Yikh, see Ikh.	
Yokaash, definition of	247
— Yum, definition of	234
Yucay, highland-eunuchs from	37
Zac and ak symbols compared	249
—, phonetic value of	250
— symbol discussed	251

	Page
Zacatlan symbol in Mexican pictography	344
Zacuzy, a Zapotec goddess	305
Zapotec and Oaxacan terms compared	282
—, day names of the	206
— forms, interpretation of	312
Zeue-cmil, meaning of	259
Zeutao, feathers, shield obtained from	46
Zero day symbol discussed	229
Zil, explanation of the name	255
— month symbol in the codices	245
Zo-daan, definition of	258
Zoo symbol in Maya hieroglyphs	235
Zoomorphic deities	22
Zotz symbol in Maya hieroglyphs	236
Zotzimil mentioned in Popol Vuh	164
Zotzuy, definition of	260
Zoo symbol in Dresden codex	235
Zuñi, a many-storied pueblo	135
—, character of masonry of	141
—, farming villages of	33, 255